SOCIETY
AND THE SCHOOLS

COMMUNICATION CHALLENGE TO
EDUCATION AND SOCIAL WORK

Robert H. Beck, Editor

*Report of the Conference on Interprofessional
Communication: Challenge to Social Work and
Education* *Co-sponsored by the National
Association of Social Workers and the
Council on Social Work Education* ■

Chicago, Illinois ■ *April 26–30, 1964*

National Association of Social Workers
2 Park Avenue, New York, N. Y. 10016

This project was supported by a grant from the National Institute of Mental Health, U.S. Public Health Service

 3

FOREWORD

In April 1964, at the Center for Continuing Education, University of Chicago, a conference was held to study problems in communication between the fields of education and social work.

The idea for such a conference was originally developed by the Education Committee of the School Social Work Section (now the Council on Social Work in Schools) of the National Association of Social Workers.[1] This committee recognized that it was essential to find more effective ways of collaborating between the professions of education and social work if the needs of the many school children who are unable to utilize educational opportunities fully because of social, emotional, and cultural problems are to be met. It seemed apparent that efforts to bring about more effective professional relationships between education and social work needed to be tackled at all levels of practice but that the foundation for such collaborative work should begin in the professional education period in both professions.

The Council on Social Work in Schools of the National Association of Social Workers in collaboration with the Council on Social Work Education co-sponsored this Conference on Interprofessional Communication for a selected group of participants interested in the implications for professional education of the problems in com-

---

[1] The Education Committee included Joseph P. Hourihan, Professor, School of Social Work, Wayne State University; Jerry L. Kelley, Assistant Dean and Assistant Professor, School of Social Work, University of Washington; Horace W. Lundberg, Dean, Graduate School of Social Service Administration at Arizona State University; John C. Nebo, Consultant in School Social Work, Division of Special Education, Illinois Office of the Superintendent of Public Instruction; Louise C. Spence, District Administrator and Supervisor of District Services, Division of Children and Youth, State Department of Public Welfare, Wisconsin; and Jane Wille, Associate Professor, The Jane Addams Graduate School of Social Work, University of Illinois and Chairman of the Education Committee. Staff assistance to the Education Committee was given by Marjorie J. Herzig, National Association of Social Workers.

munication between education and social work. Funds were obtained from the National Institute of Mental Health for this project. The thirty-nine people who participated in the conference were, with a few exceptions, deans and faculty members from colleges of education and schools of social work representing eighteen universities. The participants were almost equally divided between the fields of education and social work.

The over-all aims of the conference were (1) to identify communication problems common to the two professions and problems of interprofessional communication in general; (2) to search out means of resolving some of the major problems; and (3) to provide materials that could be expected to further the development of valid communication between social work and education.

A Conference Planning Committee was appointed with the task of developing a plan for this conference that would achieve these aims.[2] The planning committee approached the question of interprofessional communication from three points of reference: (1) the values, objectives, and functions of the professions of education and social work; (2) the objectives and major content areas in the professional education of teachers and social workers; and (3) principles of communication. Papers on these subjects, distributed for study by the conference participants prior to the conference itself, appear as Part I of this publication.

Part II of this publication contains an account of the conference discussion. The participants in the conference used the content of the papers appearing in Part I as a springboard into two days of lively discussion of problems in communication between the two professions and new ground was broken as the participants began thinking together about these problems. On the third day, the participants separated into three smaller groups where they discussed three topics that seemed particularly significant to explore in greater depth. These topics were (1) the similarities and differences in values and goals of the two professions and their implications for content in the professional education of teachers and social workers; (2) the similarities and differences in values and goals of the two professions

---

[2] The Conference Planning Committee was composed of Robert H. Beck, Professor, History and Philosophy of Education, College of Education, University of Minnesota, conference leader and editor of this publication; Dan H. Cooper, Professor of Educational Administration, School of Education, University of Michigan; Joseph P. Hourihan, Professor, School of Social Work, Wayne State University; Kenneth W. Kindelsperger, Dean, Raymond A. Kent School of Social Work, University of Louisville; Florence Poole, Professor, The Jane Addams Graduate School of Social Work, University of Illinois, and chairman, Conference Planning Committee; Mildred Sikkema, Consultant on Educational Standards, Council on Social Work Education, and Barbara M. Moore, Associate Director, Department of Social Work Practice, National Association of Social Workers.

in relation to the analysis of the various systems wherein education and social work interact; and (3) the similarities and differences in values and goals between social work and education within the school and/or the community.

The conference terminated with a presentation of "The Challenge to the Two Professions" by Samuel H. Popper, Associate Professor, Educational Administration, College of Education, University of Minnesota. This paper comprises Part III.

Special thanks and appreciation go to Robert H. Beck, conference leader and editor, and to Barbara Moore, Associate Director, Department of Social Work Practice, NASW, and Mildred Sikkema, Consultant on Educational Standards, CSWE, for their fine leadership and guidance, and to all the participants in this conference who gave so generously of themselves as authors of papers, as discussion leaders, discussants of the papers, and recorders.

Sincere thanks and appreciation also go to Judith A. Auerbach, associate editor, NASW Department of Publications, and Stella Bloch Hanau, editorial consultant, who jointly prepared this publication, and to Beatrice Saunders, director of publications at NASW, for her guidance and support.

FLORENCE POOLE

Jane Addams Graduate School of Social Work
University of Illinois
July 1965

CONTENTS

part **I**

THE TWO
PROFESSIONS

1

THE SOCIAL WORK PROFESSION

By Werner W. Boehm

In a discussion of social work purposes, there is a risk of presenting either a detailed outline or of dealing with some facets more thoroughly than with others. In presenting this paper, there is no choice but to develop some ideas in more detail since the topic is too complex and some aspects of it too unevenly developed to arrive at a balanced presentation.

To arrive at a meaningful dialogue between educators and social workers, there is a need to do more than merely report the functions of the school social worker. Rather, the purposes of the social work profession must be identified in general and these purposes must be sufficiently valid for any field of practice. Thus, when the purposes of social work are examined in the context of school social work they must be valid for that field as well as for the other fields of practice.

In addition, the task here is to describe not only the purposes social work presently seeks to achieve; those purposes that social work strives to achieve must also be presented, even if only dimly perceived. These emergent purposes can be discovered as one looks at unusual or novel social work activities; some of them existed in the statements of social work philosophy and in the commitments to which social work has been dedicated by exhortation perhaps more than by action. Thus, purposes encompass not only what social work is currently doing, but also what social work might be doing.

The term "purpose" is often equated with the terms "goal" and "function." In order to avoid confusion it is wise both to differentiate among these terms and indicate their relationship. The term "purpose" will be used here differently from the term "goal." "Goal" signifies an ultimately desired outcome; "purpose" refers to broad areas of professional intentions. The term can be viewed, although it is still general, as a specification of the term "goal."

Frequently associated with the term "purpose" is the term "function." This term is used here to indicate specific aims or categories of aims that social work seeks to achieve. To put it differently, function is a specification of purpose and points to the ways in which purposes are reached. The term "method," frequently associated with function, in turn is a specification of function and more precisely than function denotes a systematic ordering of certain characteristic professional activities grouped according to their appropriateness or use.

In the following discussion the major premises of social work goals and purposes will be outlined, and an attempt will be made to conceptualize social work purposes, functions, and methods. Finally some implications of social work purposes for communication between education and social work will be discussed.

Many of these formulations are tentative and require further thought and study. They reflect analyses of current work and have been influenced by reports of the Commission on Practice of the National Association of Social Workers, the Council on Social Work Education, writings of individual scholars both here and abroad, and practice developments reflecting new patterns of service, such as Mobilization For Youth, urban planning, urban renewal, community mental health programs, and neighborhood development plans.

Major Premises of Social Work

The purposes of social work are predicated upon and fashioned by two premises: (1) the way social work conceives of the relationship between man and society, and (2) the way social work defines its relationship to society.

MAN AND SOCIETY

The relationship between man and society may be expressed in the following statements:

1. Each person has the right to self-fulfillment, deriving from his inherent capacity and thrust toward that goal.

2. Each person has the obligation, as a member of society, to seek ways of self-fulfillment that contribute to the common good.

3. Society has the obligation to facilitate the self-fulfillment

of the individual and the right to enrichment through the contributions of its individual members.

4. Each person requires for the harmonious development of his powers socially provided and socially safeguarded opportunities for satisfying his basic needs in the physical, psychological, economic, cultural, aesthetic, and spiritual realms.

5. As society becomes more complex and interdependent, increasingly specialized social organization is required to facilitate the individual's efforts at self-realization. Although conflicts between individuals and society can never be entirely absent, social organization should be such as to reduce them to a minimum. A conception of the individual and society as interdependent leads to the view that just as it is the responsibility of society to provide appropriate social resources, it is the right of the individual to promote changes in social resources which do not serve his need-meeting efforts. Concomitantly, it is the individual's obligation to satisfy his individual needs as much as possible in ways that contribute to the enrichment of society.

6. To permit both self-realization and contribution to society by the individual, social organization must make available socially sanctioned and socially provided devices for needs satisfaction as wide in range, variety, and quality as the general welfare allows.[1]

. . . .

It must be emphasized, however, that the responsibility of social work to society as a whole by no means endows it with a set of values identical at every point with those predominating in society. The values identifiable and operative in any society are often conflicting. This profession, like any other section of society, must make some selection among them. The pressure for conformity, often identified as increasingly characteristic of our present society, has not supplanted the emphasis upon diversity valued through all our history. Social work should and does adopt what may often be unpopular positions. In the light of its own selection and interpretation of certain values which other sections of society may view differently, social work may also serve as the conscience of society.[2]

SOCIAL WORK AND AMERICAN SOCIETY

Any society creates a profession in keeping with a societal need. It entrusts a profession with certain missions that contribute to society's maintenance and further development. Hence, to understand the purposes of the social work profession American society must be understood. Perhaps these characteristics are typical of society today: the expansion of knowledge, the rapidity of techno-

---

[1] Werner W. Boehm, "The Nature of Social Work," *Social Work*, Vol. 3, No. 2 (April 1958), p. 12.

[2] *Ibid.*, p. 11.

logical change manifested particularly by automation, the shift in the proportion of aged and young in the population, the uncertain position of the United States as a political power in the world, and the uncertainty experienced by many regarding the nature of their individual identity and their role in society.

In all periods and cultures, members of society perform multiple social roles. Characteristic of modern society is increased difficulty for its members in perceiving the nature of their various and multiplying social roles and their increasing inability to perform those roles in accordance with socially sanctioned and personally desired norms.

As the economy has changed from one of scarcity to one of abundance, economic means are now available to meet man's basic needs in the economic sphere and thus to permit a shift in social concern and increased attention to man's needs in the social, emotional, and spiritual realms. In the United States, economic needs persist, although to a lesser degree than formerly. Inadequate income, inadequate housing and living conditions, inadequate health, and inadequate educational facilities continue to claim the attention of social workers and others. Available economic means, however, put American society in a better position to deal with these problems, and perhaps even to eliminate them. The inability to eliminate poverty, therefore, reflects a failure of economic and social policy rather than a failure in the creation of an adequate supply of goods and services. At the same time, the United States is in a position to pay attention to other problems of social living and focus on the satisfaction of emotional, aesthetic, and spiritual needs that begin to assume greater prominence as the material needs of significant segments of the population are satisfied or recognized as satisfiable. One of the characteristics of social living today seems to be the coexistence of subsistence requirements and aspiration requirements for the "good" life. The former are largely in the economic realm and in contrast to the past are capable of attainment. The latter have to do with style of life and are largely in the psychosocial realm. These are not yet fully understood and cannot be adequately met.

The coexistence of these requirements also suggests that in the near future the same persons may at one and the same time, or certainly within a short span of years, show the impact of both subsistence and aspiration problems. Certainly the existence in the population of large segments who are primarily concerned with aspiration problems points the way for those afflicted primarily with subsistence problems to become concerned with aspiration and the better things of life. The latter concern can be an index that they have achieved at least the basic requirements for effective functioning, such as adequate income, housing, health, and education. It seems clear that to

live effectively in modern society more is needed than the fulfillment of these basic requirements. The social changes mentioned
above, their rapidity and their nature, threaten people with role
impairment and "functionlessness," and demand socially provided
resources, or "social utilities" to facilitate their effective functioning.
While this discussion may be valid for the cultures of the United
States and Canada, it is only an application of a more general view
that presents a rationale for social work in any culture. This general
view may be expressed as follows:

> Social workers are concerned with meeting basic human needs
> in the social realm. This concern is viewed not as an end goal
> of social work but rather as a means to an end. This position
> is based on the view that the satisfaction of basic human need
> is an essential condition for the attainment of human dignity
> and constitutes a necessary basis for individual self-fulfillment,
> the goal of social work as well as of other professions. The ex-
> pression of basic human needs and the content of living are
> culturally conditioned. They vary from society to society, from
> time to time, and within societies may vary from group to
> group. . . .
> Such a view of social need would lead to a concept of social
> work activities as ongoing and essential for the effective func-
> tioning of individuals and groups in society. This view also
> implies that social workers will shift their focus of professional
> activities to new needs as they arise from the ever faulty inter-
> action between individuals and social institutions.[3]

This point of view reflects the emergence of an "institutional" perspective toward social welfare, in contrast to the "residual" perspective
held until recently by many social workers. The institutional approach postulates that in modern society social institutions are interdependent because social needs and problems are interdependent
and no one social institution can expect to attain its goals without
the participation of other co-ordinate social institutions. The residual philosophy would invoke social work only after failure has
occurred in attainment of their goals by such basic institutions as
family, economy, church, and so on. The residual perspective tends
to reflect, as Kahn has pointed out, a somewhat puritanical view and
has led to the emphasis in social work on clinical purposes to the
exclusion or neglect of purposes related to structural change.[4] The
residual approach is at least ambiguous, if not ambivalent, with

---

[3] Werner W. Boehm, *The Plan for the Social Work Curriculum Study*, document 6–70–12 (New York: Council on Social Work Education, 1956), p. 36. Quoted
in Boehm, *op. cit.*, pp. 12–13.

[4] Alfred J. Kahn, "Investment in People," a social work perspective paper presented at the Urban Studies Center, Rutgers—The State University, November
1963. (Mimeographed.)

reference to whether or not services that anyone needs are to be available to him as a matter of right. As Kahn suggests, the institutional view "takes account of technological and social changes which alter the relationships of man both to primary institutions and to the general social environment. New social 'inventions' appear in response to the functional prerequisite of life in this changed social environment and they are as 'normal' in their way, in their relationship to these changed circumstances, as were the originally developed primary social institutions of a primitive agricultural economy." [5]

The user of these new social inventions is no more dependent and shows no more evidence of individual or familial incapacity than is the modern citizen who relies upon the existence of an effective and efficient health, fire, and police department in order to go about his business. "Social utilities" then are as much a requirement for effective living as are the public services of a modern community.

Purposes of Social Work

The goal of social work is the "enhancement of social functioning wherever the need for such enhancement is either socially or individually perceived." [6] The two premises discussed above contain social work purposes by implication. To make the purposes of social work explicit enables one both to specify social work goals and thereby to differentiate them from the goals of other professions. Social work cannot possibly claim a monopoly on the enhancement of social functioning and must specify those purposes and functions through which characteristically it seeks to reach the goal of enhancement of social functioning. The purposes of social work are social habilitation and social restoration.

SOCIAL HABILITATION

In general terms social habilitation seeks to equip the total population or significant segments of it with those social resources and programs essential for their functioning. For example, it appears that role performance norms for a variety of age groups, particularly the aged and adolescents, either are obscure or entirely missing.

Social habilitation involves the creation of services that provide information and opportunity for such role activities. In a similar vein, services could be (and to some extent already have been) created whereby role requirements for family living would be made available, taking into consideration differentials in the stage of family cycle as well as ethnic and socioeconomic differences. Another example is the provision of services enabling people to learn

---

[5] *Ibid.*
[6] Boehm, "The Nature of Social Work," *op. cit.*, p. 13.

16

about the legal provisions to which they are entitled, opportunities to learn the requirements of new roles (e.g., when moving from a rural to an urban setting or when moving from one socioeconomic level to another).

Another area of social habilitation is the creation or provision of resources needed for the solution of large unsolved social problems which affect significant segments of the population. Currently, habilitation is needed for those members of society who are the victims of poverty, whose education is substandard, whose backgrounds deprive them of equality of opportunity in educational and vocational endeavors, or who are victims of discrimination.

Social habilitation as a purpose of social work seeks to deal with two types of social problems that characterize contemporary society: (1) the instrumental, survival, or subsistence problems; and (2) the noninstrumental, self-fulfillment, or aspiration problems. Through social habilitation social work seeks to provide answers to three important questions: Whose bellies should be filled? What kind of life do people want to live? What kind of society will foster that life? Thus the poor and the old, the young and the unskilled, the minority and the majority, the women and the disabled, all would be encompassed in programs of social habilitation.

The scope of this purpose is formidable and naturally questions arise. How is the purpose of habilitation achieved? What functions are appropriate for that purpose? Although the classification which follows may be somewhat forced, the current description of professional activities suggests the existence, actual and potential, of two functions: (1) planned change in the social structure of our society; and (2) planned change in the organizational and program pattern of social welfare resources.

The social structure. Here social work would operate according to the premises that the individual and society are interdependent and that society has an obligation to provide the means that enable individual members of society to obtain self-fulfillment. Social work would therefore not be limited to problems that have a clear-cut social welfare component, such as inadequate assistance payments or inadequate unemployment compensation. Rather social work would intervene in any social problem whose existence is apt to lead to impairment of social functioning or thwart the unfolding of individual potential. The great social questions of the day whose solutions appear to require changes in existing social institutions—the economy, the family, the educational system, or the political structure—warrant the participation of social work. However, since other groups in society may have similar interests and concerns, social work will find itself allied with or will seek the alliance of other professions and political forces in the pursuit of this goal.

17

The Two Professions

Social work has traditionally been committed to the achievement of this purpose but in its practice has not given much emphasis to it. C. Wright Mills, in a paper significantly entitled "The Professional Ideology of Social Pathologists," was critical of the predominant emphasis in social work (and elsewhere) on situational aspects of social problems and deplored its failure to view flaws in the social structure as contributing to pathological situations.

> Present institutions train several types of persons—such as judges and social workers—to think in terms of "situation." Their activities and mental outlook are set within the existent norms of society; in their professional work they tend to have an occupationally trained incapacity to rise above series of "cases." It is in part through such concepts as "situation" and through such methods as "the case approach" that social pathologists have been intellectually tied to social work with its occupational position and political limitations. And, again, the similarity of origin and the probable lack of any continuous "class experience" of the group of thinkers decreases their chances to see social structures rather than a scatter of situations.[7]

A similar distinction, although not a sharp critique of the situational approach is being attempted by DeJongh who differentiates between social welfare activities and social work activities and defines the former as those which indicate "the broad concept encompassing any activity of individuals and groups and communities to improve the quality of our social life." [8] He would limit the term "social work" to the activities around specific problems requiring special competence.

Recent developments here in the United States and the work of the United Nations with developing countries have sharpened sensitivity to flaws in the social structure. Certainly, there are striking differences between the United States on one hand and such countries as the Congo, Vietnam, and Indonesia on the other. The problems that confront American society today are often of a different order altogether. Closer inspection, however, suggests that these differences are not differences in kind but in degree. American society too, has its structural shortcomings and they become increasingly evident as attempts are made to deal with megalopolis; to redefine and reshape the relationship between the federal government, the states, and the localities; and to re-examine the efficacy of the democratic process in the face of the ubiquitous requirements for technical proficiency and

---

[7] C. Wright Mills, "The Professional Ideology of Social Pathologists," *American Journal of Sociology*, Vol. 49, No. 2 (September 1943), p. 171.

[8] A. F. DeJongh, "The Function of Social Work," a paper delivered at the 10th International Conference of Social Work, Rome, Italy, 1961. (Mimeographed.)

the essential participation of the expert. It appears that American society is not capable of achieving both a cohesive and a pluralistic culture that succeeds in binding all segments of the populations regardless of class, caste, and ethnic membership while at the same time permitting differentiation for these groups within the larger unit. The society seems impotent in the face of overcrowding and population concentration in limited space to help with the emergence of styles and standards of life which reflect incorporation of value and permit expression of vitality. Lastly, intensive participation of the United States in the world community inevitably produces conditions and events in the political and economic realms that wreak changes, imperceptible perhaps, but changes nevertheless, which affect the way of life and the mode of thinking and feeling of individuals, families, and groups.

A new world reality begins to fashion a new world view. As people come to observe and then to understand this new reality, they become aware that habitual modes of explanation fall short of the mark, as do habitual ways of action.

The pattern of social welfare resources. This function is more in keeping with some traditional social work concerns although the methods are not likely to be completely identical with currently used ones. Essentially, planned change in this sphere includes program development, program change, enhancement of organizational capabilities, and provision of opportunities through organizational means.

Program development refers to the creation of new programs that correspond to new needs. Examples include the Citizens Advice Bureaus in Great Britain and Mobilization For Youth in New York, the development of urban renewal programs, the rise of patterns of service whereby groups such as migratory workers and dislocated families can be effectively reached, and the creation of new patterns of personnel deployment that stretch the scope and improve the quality of services.

Program change refers to modification of existing, more or less traditional social welfare programs, through expansion, merger, shift in emphasis, or through addition of new programs. Here belong the experimental programs with migratory workers, the new patterns of day care, and the expansion of homemaker and home-helper programs in public and voluntary welfare agencies.

Enhancement of organizational capability and opportunity for service provision refers to modification of organizational structures as a result of analysis and in the light of recognition that a different organizational pattern from the one developed to meet the social needs of the country in 1900 is more likely to meet current requirements. Increasingly, organizational theory seems to provide insights into the relationship between the program and the user of the program. An increase in facilities is not always the best answer and different organizational arrangements may facilitate moving beyond only a segment of the population to reaching all those who are potential users of a given social welfare program.

SOCIAL RESTORATION

In an analogy with medicine social habilitation may be equated with the public health purpose of medicine, and social restoration with the clinical purpose of medicine. As in medicine some of the clinical clientele is identical with the public health clientele but it is necessary to determine the problems for which the clinical purpose of social work is particularly appropriate.

This is the most specific area of social work. It is here that the professional comes in direct contact with the user of service. In performing the function of planned structural or organizational change, the intervention is primarily on a social action or social reform level. By contrast, two large categories of problems fall within the purview of social restoration. One comprises the result of the instrumental or survival problems of individuals, families, and groups in modern life and the other the result of self-fulfillment or aspiration problems of man in modern society, especially in American society, where self-fulfillment is most highly valued.

The instrumental or survival problems of modern life include the consequences or impact on the social functioning of individuals, families, and groups of such unsolved social problems as poverty, inadequate education, deficiencies in vocational training, discrimination, and poor health.

The noninstrumental or self-fulfillment problems are related to the difficulties in social relationships that occur in modern society because of identity diffusion, because of the nonattainment of or dissatisfaction with style of life in the emotional, aesthetic, and spiritual realms. They include impairment of family functioning as evidenced in parent-child difficulties and husband-wife relations, impairment of civic functioning in relation to state and nation. In this category belong mild or acute impairment of role performance which many individuals in our modern society currently experience, whether the impaired role is that of student, parent, sibling, employee, or citizen. Here also belong general identity problems and the difficulties many persons experience in the performance of family, peer, and civic roles. In general, these are the "existential" problems that have been identified as being typical of the times. While social role impairment may also be a symptom of instrumental problems, the common denominator of problems in this category is the absence of any instrumental deficiency. Social work has traditionally assumed an important place in dealing with the consequences of social problems but has not tended to consider them as natural consequences of modern living.

There are four groups of clients for whom the clinical social work purpose of social restoration is appropriate. One group consists of those who show the impact of unsolved social problems. Among these are the victims of poverty, unemployment (structural unemployment caused by technological changes such as automation or seasonal and transitory unemployment), and racial discrimination. Also included here are the school dropouts and those with marginal incomes, inadequate housing, and the like. These are often the persons who have been defeated, who have given up or lost motivation, and who have as a result of these unsolved social problems suffered severe impairment of social functioning.

Another group of clients for whom restoration is appropriate are the people whose social functioning is impaired, not because of the absence of socially provided resources that would obviate or alleviate social problems, but rather because the available social resources are inadequate or have not been in operation long enough to be effective or generally known. In some instances a lag occurs between the period of time when a set of resources becomes available and the time when they are actually used. Sometimes inadequate or insufficient information deprives the potential users of actually available resources.

Another group of clients includes those who do not find access to actually existing resources. In this category belong not only the persons who lack knowledge of existing resources but also those who are denied resources because they are victims of discriminatory practices.

The fourth category of clients is comprised of those who know of the existence of resources and would avail themselves of them, but lack the social, intellectual, and emotional skills, or the "interpersonal competence" to make use of the existing resources. Hence, they suffer from impairment of social functioning. These are the individuals, families, and groups who suffer frequently from psychosocial disabilities inherent in their personalities and their relationships and in this category belong highly disorganized families and persons, and families with psychological disabilities.

It is obvious that these four categories of clients are not mutually exclusive. Re-enforcement of impairment of social functioning can occur because any one client may share the characteristics of several of these four groups. Resource disability, resource deficiency, or inaccessibility to resources coupled with psychosocial disabilities inherent in persons and families tends to re-enforce the impairment of social functioning.

Functions and Methods of Social Work

The meaning of social habilitation and social restoration becomes clearer when they are viewed in the context of the functions of social work, which are defined as restoration, provision, and prevention.[9] The three concepts can be described as follows:

1. *Restoration.* This function seeks to identify and control or eliminate those factors in the interactional process that have caused a breakdown or impairment of social relationships. It aims at a return to a maximum level of functioning. This function may be seen as curative and rehabilitative. Its curative aspects are to eliminate factors that have caused breakdown of functioning, and its rehabilitative aspects to reorganize and rebuild interactional patterns.

2. *Provision of Resources.* This function entails the creation, enrichment, improvement, and better co-ordination of social resources and the mobilization of existing, but inoperative, individual capacity for interaction in the physical, intellectual, emotional, or spiritual realms. This function may be seen as developmental and educational. Its developmental aspects are designed to further the effectiveness of existing social resources or bring to full flower personal capacity for more effective social interaction. Its educational aspects are designed to acquaint the public (including recipients of service) with specific conditions and needs for new or changed social resources. Also involved is leadership in determining and applying principles by which this function can be carried out. This function derives its rationale from the socially sanctioned nature of social work which obligates the profession to contribute to the welfare of the community.

3. *Prevention.* This function entails early discovery, control, and elimination of conditions and situations that potentially could hamper effective social functioning. The following subdivisions may be identified:

a. Prevention of problems in the area of interaction between individuals and groups: This is designed to eliminate or control and to follow up individual or environmental factors in interaction that may cause problems to occur, to recur, or to be aggravated; to anticipate and take precautions about "tender areas" where problems may occur.

---

[9] This formulation first occurred in Werner W. Boehm, *The Plan for the Social Work Curriculum Study,* document 6–70–12 (New York: Council on Social Work Education, 1956). It was further developed and incorporated in a paper by Boehm, "The Nature of Social Work," *Social Work,* Vol. 3, No. 2 (April 1958), pp. 10–18; and at about the same time a similar formulation was developed by Alfred J. Kahn, "The Function of Social Work in the Modern World," in Kahn, ed., *Issues in American Social Work* (New York: Columbia University Press, 1959), pp. 3–38.

b. Prevention of social ills: This is designed to collect and interpret data on the incidence and predictability of problems in interaction. In combination with related aspects of the function of provision, this aspect of prevention contributes to the creation of social health. In pursuing it, much may be learned about "social infection" and "social contamination" which will contribute to the further development of both functions.[10]

This formulation, prepared in 1958, can be somewhat revised in the light of subsequent developments, especially because of the scrutiny of fields of practice by the Council on Social Work Education and the National Association of Social Workers, and recent writings by Harriett M. Bartlett and Alfred J. Kahn. It appears that the trinity of functions can be maintained, but it is also clear that the purposes and functions of social work can be made more specific and aspects of the earlier formulation that were only implied or not clearly delineated can now be developed further.

In 1958 it appeared that in practice the three functions of social work were not entirely separable. Activities carried on in relation to any given problem in interaction may simultaneously have restorative, preventive, and provisional functions, or may have implications for one while emphasizing another. It has now become possible to expand the somewhat elliptical meaning of that formulation.

Generally, unmet needs in society create problems for individuals and families. Hence the social habilitation purpose which seeks to deal with pervasive social problems is preventive. In the sense that it keeps social problems from occurring, it achieves primary prevention. This function is analogous to the public health function in medicine. Social work is not alone in performing it, but can be associated in its performance with other professions and groups including public health personnel, educators, lawyers, economists, and politicians. What Kahn has called "developmental provision" is one of the major means whereby social problems are met in society. For example, a change in income distribution might transform an estimated thirty million persons in American society from victims of poverty and relief recipients into "paying customers." They would become users of service rather than remain clients. Massive programs of retraining and rehabilitation might cause some of them to perform in keeping with their intellectual and emotional equipment and enable them to carry out roles in an automated society that demand a high level of both social and vocational skill. However, there will always be a segment of the

---

[10] Boehm, "The Nature of Social Work," *op. cit.*, pp. 16–17.

population that will not be capable of performing adequately because of certain inherent limitations either in their personal equipment or because of handicaps residing in their immediate social and cultural situation. For these persons the social restoration purpose of social work must be invoked.

SOCIAL HABILITATION

Enhancing the capability or the potential of existing social institutions such as the economy or education to carry out their societal functions more effectively requires review, clarification, and possibly change of institutional specifications and steps appropriate for the attainment of this function. The methods include activities concerned with planning for new resources and co-ordination of existing resources with the newly created ones, or the development of better organization and co-ordination of these resources. Assessment of the adequacy and appropriateness of existing programs, of existing policies, and the effectiveness and appropriateness of current planning may also be needed. In some instances it will be necessary to engage in what may be called anticipatory planning or planning that is designed to forestall the emergence of social problems. An example of this kind of activity would be the planning that has begun to identify the measures needed to cope with the social and psychological, as well as the technological consequences of automation. Such planning may require not only the expert in various social and economic fields, but also the participation of representatives of the political machinery, and alliance with thinkers and philosophers who are keen observers of the social scene.

In sum, the social habilitation purpose has primary preventive and provisional functions. The direction of this function is social change either in the social structure or the structure of the social services. The activities leading to such change are apt to lead to a different kind of society. Traditional community organization skills are needed for these activities. In addition, there is need for skills that have not yet been fully defined in social work practice and therefore are not readily taught in social work education. These skills might be termed social welfare policy skills. They are not identical with the skills of the typical community organizer or the typical administrator of a social welfare program although some of the skills possessed by these persons may well belong here.

The method that the social worker uses in carrying out this function might be called social system intervention. It involves assessing the adequacy and the appropriateness of existing social programs and policies in the light of emerging needs. The required skills may include social need assessment, social resource analysis, policy formulation, policy implementation, and the like. The mode of attack would be systematic and would include assessment, planning and implementation of plan, evaluation of outcome, and would involve collaboration with other professions, other groups in society, including politicians, planners, as well as representatives of the public.

SOCIAL RESTORATION

Two functions seem appropriate for social restoration: rehabilitation and alleviation. The rehabilitative function seeks to help individuals, families and groups to reach at least a previous level of functioning—a level that existed before the disability or social problem that resulted in impairment of social functioning. This rehabilitative function may seek, however, not only to produce a previous level of functioning, but also to increase the level of functioning to a point higher than it was prior to impairment.

The alleviative function is essentially therapeutic. It seeks to eliminate those factors in the situation that stand in the way of a return to a higher level of social functioning. This level may not be as high as was the level which existed prior to the onset of the problem, but alleviation is designed to bring about the optimum level the person or the family or the group can reach, given social structural and situational factors which cannot be changed.

Contrary to social habilitation where intervention is on the level of the social structure or large social systems, here the intervention is directed toward the individual, family, or group. Thus, while social habilitation may be characterized by social structure intervention (in large systems), social restoration may be characterized by situational intervention (in small systems). The restorative purpose is frequently associated with prevention but prevention here is secondary and tertiary in the sense that the occurrence of impairment of social functioning will be prevented or further deterioration will be avoided.

Change in the social situation of the individual, family, or group is sought through utilization of existing social welfare programs and policies as well as through the relatively well-defined skills of the professional. Situational intervention is geared to enhancing the effectiveness of role performance in the situation and may include alteration of relationships between individuals or members of the family or small groups, the immediate social circumstances and specific environmental conditions that present a relatively unique constellation of forces and factors for each individual family or group.

The professional mode of attack is systematic and involves assessment, planning, implementation, and evaluation of outcome. It relies heavily on utilization of agency function and agency program resources. It tends to be carried out within the framework of existing agency policy, the available community resources and the use of self in a professional and disciplined fashion in the context of the professional relationship. The client, or the user of service, participates in the problem-solving process and collaboration with other helping professions is frequent. Clearly, the traditional activities of the social worker come into being here much more readily. Situational intervention involves such traditional methods as casework and group work. In the future, however, identification of the situational problem, the dimensions of the situation, and the term "situational intervention" itself may foreshadow a major clinical method different from the current conceptualization of professional activities called casework and group work.

The users of the method of situational intervention might be individuals, families, and small groups, and the method itself might be characterized by some of the traditional methods and techniques developed in casework and group work with the process of interaction being clearly defined and retaining its importance and with the use of the self in a professionally disciplined fashion and the place of the professional relationship between user and professional performing a key role in this method.

In practice social habilitation and social restoration cannot be and should not be entirely separated although in traditional social work practice social restoration is much more pronounced than is social habilitation. Increasingly there is recognition in social work that both purposes are needed. Historically the social habilitation purpose has never been entirely absent from practice and it has loomed large in social work commitment.

Both purposes require systematic approaches and while they are unevenly developed, they are in existence. Both purposes require the co-operation of social workers with other groups of professionals such as educators, lawyers, physicians, and clergymen; both also require the participation of the lay public. The participation of other professions is different to some extent for each of these purposes. In relation to social habilitation, policy personnel rather than service personnel tend to be involved. Both purposes, the way they are carried out, the respective weight given them in the over-all assignment of social work manpower, and social work deployment of energy and priority distribution are affected by the perspectives the profession has of itself, of its role in society, and of its relationship with other professions.

It might also be speculated that the social work clinician may hold a view of society different from that of the social welfare politician. It is possible that the situational intervention practitioner may have a mental outlook that is set within the existing norms of society, whereas the social welfare politician may be much more concerned with assessing the adequacy and effectiveness of present social structure for meeting social needs. Hence, the social change focus may be much more pronounced in the latter than in the former.

Collaboration Between Social Workers and Educators

The pattern of collaboration and hence the mode of communication developed between professions is in large part determined by two sets of factors: (1) the functions which each profession sees itself perform, and (2) the organizational structures within which the members of the profession carry out these functions.

When it comes to the first set of criteria it is well to remember that professional activities that are inspired by the residual perspective as against those that are inspired by the institutional perspective are apt to lead to different actions on the part of the professional. If the institutional perspective prevails it is likely that the member of the social work profession, for example, in co-operation with a member of the teaching profession in a school setting sees himself much more in a partnership role than in a staff role. In that case he will seek to facilitate the function of the school as an organ of socialization through activities of a relatively well-defined nature that dovetail with those of the teacher as well as those of other personnel in the school system. To put this differently, there will be common as well as separate areas of activity and concern shared by the several professions within the school system. For instance, understanding the social, emotional, cultural, and economic factors that underlie a child's behavior in school might be called, in the words of Seward Hiltner, "the common village green" shared by the profession of education and the profession of social work, and probably also by other professional personnel in the school.[11] But where there is a "common village green" there must also be relatively distinct functions. These, in keeping with the social restoration purpose, would cause the social worker to work with the school child and in some instances also with his family toward more effective social functioning of the school child as a member of the school system or in the performance of his role as a pupil. This might entail dealing with the emotional and social problems that exist in the child's situation. It might, however, also entail examining the

---

[11] Seward Hiltner, "Tension and Mutual Support Among the Helping Professions," *Social Service Review,* Vol. 31, No. 4 (December 1957), p. 7.

social structure to determine whether it deprives the child of certain opportunities. The important consideration, however, is that the social worker perceives his function as being co-ordinate with that of the educator and that his function be also so perceived by the principal and superintendent who assign both teaching personnel and social work personnel to certain tasks. Such a view of both social worker and teacher leads to a different structural arrangement of duties in the school system from what it would be if the function of the social worker reflected a residual perspective, whether it be held by the social worker or by the school principal. The residual perspective would cause the social worker to intervene only in those instances where the educational system has failed. By contrast the institutional perspective would postulate that collaboration is taking place on the basis of the conviction shared by both educators and social workers that in a modern school a pupil requires the services of a social worker as well as those of an educator in order to function effectively. The pupil brings to his role not only his intellectual equipment but also the emotional and social circumstances of his background, which may require understanding and perhaps change if he is to perform his role effectively.

Institutional perspectives, if they prevail among both educators and social workers, lead not only to harmonious collaboration but also will augment the co-ordinated use of school and community resources. Harmony is apt to reign also when both professionals share a residual philosophy but the use they are apt to make of themselves and the school's resources is not likely to increase the pupils' social functioning. Disharmony will result if the residual perspective is held by one and the institutional perspective by another of the collaborating professions.

The pattern of collaboration and communication between the profession of social work and the profession of education in the school is also affected by the presence or absence of a social habilitation purpose. A school may consider that it is charged with carrying out society's goals, namely to socialize the young and participate with the family and other social institutions in the process of socialization. It may not address itself to the question of whether or not there are conditions in society that make socialization difficult. Juxtaposed with this conception of the school as an organ of the educational institution in society might be a conception that the school is entrusted, as are all other social institutions, with the task of social change and with the task of identifying social problems that require different structural arrangements, different institutional provisions than are extant. If the school then sees its task as contributing to social change and not merely dealing with situational factors caused by unmet social needs, then the school will perform a different role. It will engage in activities that will not only lead to clinical work or social restoration but also to social habilitation. The school will then perform the task of bringing to the attention of the political establishment or of other social institutions the impact of unmet social needs. For example, the school may call attention to the unavailability of the educational system to members of minority groups who because of social or cultural handicaps have become intellectually and emotionally unable to benefit from the school system. The school may call attention to the existence of poverty or structural unemployment, forces which, unless relieved through structural changes, hamper equal access to educational opportunities. It may also point out current inadequacies of social welfare provisions or income loss due to technological unemployment. In cases like these if a school sees itself as an organ of social change, it will perceive the functions of all its personnel, teachers and social workers included, as participating in carrying out a social habilitation purpose.

This state of affairs, if and when it comes into being, illustrates the point made earlier that in practice social restoration and social habilitation purposes are not always clearly distinguishable. In the situations described, the social restoration purpose is clearly predominant but the social habilitation purpose is noticeably present and can constitute an important aspect of the total performance.

In the field of school social work, social workers have not limited themselves to social restoration and the situational approach. A project such as Mobilization For Youth in New York City or the work done by the late Berta Fantl at Hunter's Point in San Francisco constitutes evidence.[12] These projects seek to bring about changes in the social structure by expanding the range of opportunities for pupils from lower socioeconomic and minority groups and by ingeniously creating new community agency relationships; by enlisting political and civic efforts and creating new programs geared to the unmet needs of persons, families, and groups for whom school opportunities otherwise would be meaningless.

However, intervention on the level of social structure is much less developed than intervention on the situational level. Yet for a long time there has been an awareness that the goals of the school cannot be accomplished by educational and situational endeavors alone. Now there is recognition that social work's participation is needed on several levels, the situational as well as the social structure. Such a view is likely to lead to increased collaboration not only to achieve restoration but also to achieve habilitation with collaborative in-

---

[12] Berta Fantl, "Casework in Lower Class Districts," *Mental Hygiene*, Vol. 45, No. 3 (July 1961), pp. 425–438.

volvement of professional organizations developed for and by the professions of teaching and social work. Such collaboration of necessity would be on the policy level and would clearly be concerned with social change.

The National Association of Social Workers and educational membership organizations should be able to define common interests of teachers and social workers in relation to such social problems as equality of opportunity in education or health. It is not inconceivable that social workers and educators, through their respective organizational representatives, pool their thinking and observations about flaws in the social structure, limitations in the style of life, and the great issues of modern existence. It is not inconceivable that the wisdom of teachers in the schools and the wisdom of social workers in the agencies might be fed into the educational institutions of both with a view to enhancing the quality of the professional practitioner in both education and social work. It is not inconceivable that the practice experience of teachers pooled with the practice experience of social workers will bring about more effective patterns of service in the community and make available new insights about man and society.

2

THE TEACHING PROFESSION

By Ole Sand

Like the social worker, the teacher is a practitioner, guiding the learner (or client) toward discoveries and new experiences through which his behavior is changed and modified. Good education enables the individual to function most effectively in his environment, to reach his own greatest potential, and to contribute constructively to the society in which he lives. Our schools, colleges, and professional schools are charged with the task of providing the opportunity for many of the experiences and discoveries that will accomplish such ends.[1]

Before exploring what the teaching profession contributes, and how teachers may be prepared for their task, it is perhaps appropriate to outline some of the issues and objectives of elementary and secondary education. The implications of these issues for teacher preparation can then be explored.

Americans have always valued education and have been one of the few nations to attempt to educate at public expense so many and so varied a people. There has occurred in the last fifteen years the greatest outcry in the country's history for improvements in the educational system and, indeed, it is increasingly apparent that a key to the future lies in the kind of education provided.

---

[1] The beginning portions of this paper draw heavily and often directly from the four-volume report of the NEA Project on Instruction of which the author of this paper was director. Special credit is due Dorothy Fraser, Dorothy Neubauer, Margery Thompson, John I. Goodlad, and Richard I. Miller, the other writers of the report. *See Education in a Changing Society, Deciding What to Teach, Planning and Organizing for Teaching* (Washington, D.C.: National Education Association, 1963), and *Schools for the Sixties,* a report of the NEA Project on Instruction (New York: McGraw-Hill Book Co., 1963).

Today, a special urgency dictates educational reappraisal and anticipates educational change. This urgency stems from three basic but complex sets of facts:

1. Contemporary society is changing so fundamentally and rapidly that it is often difficult for people to fit themselves into the present and project into the future. This generation and future generations must look to the schools for help in understanding, living with, and directing social change.

2. The incredible expansion of knowledge threatens to be overwhelming unless some intelligent solutions to problems created by the new and growing wealth of information are found. What knowledge to select and how to organize it for learning—these are two of the problems that require continuing attention.

3. Significant discoveries are being made about people and learning—discoveries that emphasize the vast range of differences among and within individuals and point to the great variety of ways in which people can learn. At a time when there is so much to be learned, and so urgent a need to learn it, new teaching methods must be created and old ones adapted to accelerate and enrich the teaching-learning process.

These facts of twentieth-century life create some basic problems for the instructional program of the schools. There is no shortage of ideas about what these problems are and how they should be solved. There has been a clamor of debate from all sides, often generating more heat than light.

In 1959, the National Education Association established the Project on the Instructional Program of the Public Schools to explore the problems and the possibilities for their solution. A fourteen-member national committee composed of classroom teachers, public school administrators, and university professors was appointed. From time to time, distinguished citizens and scholars in the academic disciplines served in special advisory capacities.

There was unanimous agreement among the committee members that its function was not to respond to the "critics," nor to enunciate a "national curriculum," nor to recommend the specific content to be taught in the various school subjects. Rather, the committee decided it would make the most significant contribution by identifying the critical concerns in American education and formulating recommendations about them.

Asking the Right Questions

No man is just educated; he is educated for some purpose or for many purposes. Decisions about the purposes of education and ways to achieve them are made by many people. But before good decisions can be made, the right questions must be asked, and before the right questions can be asked areas of concern must be identified. A major task of the NEA Project on Instruction was to identify the significant areas of concern, select from these areas the ones on which the project would concentrate, and then raise the right questions about them. Realistically, the framework of the project did not lend itself to thorough treatment of all the significant areas in education. Limits had to be set, with the result that certain significant concerns—pupil and teacher evaluation, teacher education, and the teaching act itself, for example—were not treated in any detail. Twelve areas of educational concern were identified and a cluster of questions about them was formulated. The questions were these:

1. Who should make what decisions about education?

2. How can an extensive program of educational research, experimentation, and innovation be developed?

3. How can the instructional program of the school be designed to develop the individual potentialities of all members of the school population within the framework of a society that values both unity and diversity?

4. What are the distinctive responsibilities of the school in contrast to those that properly belong to the family, the church, industry, and various youth-serving agencies? What responsibilities should the school share with other institutions and agencies; what should be included or excluded in the school program?

5. What is the school's role in dealing with serious national problems such as youth unemployment and juvenile delinquency?

6. What is the school's role in teaching about controversial issues and about communism and other ideologies?

7. How can the school provide a balanced program for the individual and maintain it amidst various pressures for specialization?

8. How can schools make wise selections of content from the evergrowing body of available knowledge?

9. How should the content of the curriculum be organized?

10. How should the curriculum of the school be organized to give appropriate direction to the instructional process?

11. How should the school and the classroom be organized to make the most effective use of the time and talents of students and teachers?

12. How can the quality of instructional materials be improved? How can the products of modern technology be used effectively? How can space be designed and used to support the instructional program?

Data for Decisions

Decisions cannot be made in a vacuum. The questions posed above can be resolved only on the basis of a deliberate analysis of the forces that shape education. In formulating its recommendations, the committee sought direction from three major sources: social trends and forces, knowledge of the human being as a learner, and the accumulated body of organized knowledge about the world and man. In these areas lie the forces that determine the setting and the possible method and substance of education. These forces must then be screened against the values and objectives that society sets for education, and the guides that influence the translation of what could be into what shall be.

VALUES AND OBJECTIVES

Every society is directed and sustained by a core of values that represents its ideals, standards, and norms. There are also values that are a reflection of human preferences, of what people actually want and seek to obtain. These operational values develop from personal needs and sometimes conflict with the society's normative values; what people want is not always consistent with what they believe they ought to want.

Today, the racial situation in our country points up such an inconsistency. Freedom, justice, equality have always been ideals of America. Yet, lack of freedom, injustice, and great inequalities exist in this country because personal values about race and religion, bolstered by custom and habit, override patriotic ideals.

Actual wants are modified by changes in society and culture. Today people value many things that earlier generations did not, simply because current objects of desire did not then exist as genuine possibilities. Values in terms of material comforts are quite different than they were before the fruits of mass production and technology were available. Values in terms of attitudes and behavior will change as more and more people, Negro and white, recognize that traditional roles cannot forever be maintained comfortably.

Educational values should reflect the generally accepted ideals of society. Standards of what ought to be should be a guide to both teaching and learning. Equally necessary, educational values should reflect the needs and interests of the learner. Education must comprehend what it is before it can broaden and relate the immediate to the ideal. The educator's task is to build continuity between the interests of the learner and the standards of excellence that transcend the immediate desires of the immature.

The values against which the multiple possibilities for educational practice are screened must be made explicit. To do otherwise would be to make decisions without reference to what is sought and without sufficient heed to the actual needs of those at whom the values are aimed. The following values are vital as criteria for assessing present practices and as guides to future improvement of the schools: (1) respect for the worth and dignity of every individual; (2) equality of opportunity for all children; (3) encouragement of variability; (4) faith in man's ability to make rational decisions; (5) shared responsibility for the common good; and (6) respect for moral and spiritual values, and ethical standards of conduct.

The schools should not and cannot provide all of the learning opportunities that students need in order to live fully and effectively. Other agencies have particular responsibilities in the education of youth and learning also takes place outside the school and continuously throughout life. Furthermore, school time and facilities are finite, making it impossible as well as undesirable that the schools be the source for all necessary learning.

Education is a process of changing behavior—behavior in the broad sense of thinking, feeling, and acting. As a result of education, students should acquire ideas they did not have, skills they did not possess, interests broader and more mature than they had known, and ways of thinking more effective than they had employed. From this viewpoint, educational objectives should be stated in terms of behavorial change, and the responsibilities of the schools should be identified with the behavioral changes most susceptible of accomplishment by the schools rather than by other educative agencies. It is necessary for the schools to choose relatively few important objectives, to work toward them consistently, and to review them periodically in the light of changing times. The additive approach of putting more subject matter into the curriculum and adopting a multitude of educational goals is ineffective.

The basic criterion in establishing priorities should be an assessment of the contributions that education can make to the individual, to society, and to the improvement of mankind. In this swift-moving world, such choices are not easy. What knowledge will today's ten-year-old need three decades hence? What skills will he require to live successfully? What problems will he have to solve? In what social context will he need to reinterpret basic human values? Education must help the individual to cope with change as well as to maintain values that are relatively constant.

The essential objectives of education, therefore, must be premised on a recognition that education is a process of changing behavior and that a changing society requires the capacity for self-teaching and self-adaptation. Priorities in educational objectives should be placed upon such goals as:

1. Learning how to learn, how to attack new problems, and how to acquire new knowledge.
2. Using rational processes.
3. Building competence in basic skills.
4. Developing intellectual and vocational competence.

35

5. Exploring values in new experience.
6. Understanding concepts and generalizations.

Above all, the school must develop in the pupil the ability to learn under his own initiative and an abiding interest in doing so.

SOCIETY AS A BASE

Social forces such as science and technology, economic growth, large bureaucratic organizations, leisure time, television and other mass media, urbanization, population growth, and international interdependence and conflict, affect the lives of students profoundly.

An intelligent awareness of them is only a beginning toward shaping them to positive rather than negative effects. The schools cannot correct housing patterns, employment practices, and discriminatory voting registration laws any more than they can alter the bitter residue of other nations' colonial policies or call back the scientific discoveries that presage man's control or destruction of nature. But the schools can help students to gain a knowledge of the world in which they find themselves, with a more complete history of all its cultures and as many possible solutions to its problems as can now be foreseen. This much, at the very least, the schools can and should do.

THE LEARNER AS A BASE

Every child has an inner push to become a more complete person and to learn what can become meaningful to him. The art of teaching lies in stimulating this force and in keeping it alive, free, and developing. To do so, it is essential to understand the learner, to know what he is working on, what he is up against, and what his basic assets include.

Investigations by psychologists during the last fifteen years have provided much significant information about thinking, learning, and personality. Their findings are helping to lay a better foundation for changes in curriculum and methods of teaching. It seems clear now that development is achieved through learning, probably constrained by biochemical processes that may be genetically regulated. The idea of development as emergence according to a precise timetable is withering on the vine. No one child develops or learns at the exact rate of another, nor is a child's own learning all of a piece; differences exist within individuals as well as among them.

Some of the concerns that seem most significant in educational planning and practice, in terms of the learner, are: acknowledging differences within the individual; acknowledging differences among individuals; acknowledging social group differences; recognizing and nurturing creativity; promoting the development of responsibility; promoting the development of positive self-attitudes; relating learning to development in children; and evaluating the learner's motivations.

ORGANIZED KNOWLEDGE AS A BASE

Probably the most immediate single factor forcing change upon education is the explosion of knowledge—the "information revolution." Furthermore, because scientific and scholarly work is now quite extensive and many people are engaged in it, the rate of revision is swift. Teaching the disciplines in this situation clearly requires teaching something more permanent and pervasive than a catalog of factual knowledge, although some facts are essential, and it is clear that there is a continuing need for drill and repetition for learning of basic information.

Educators are not only concerned with the amount of knowledge students possess but also with students' lack of understanding about what they presumably know. Since 1955, a vivid awareness of this latter problem has led some scholars and researchers to explore ways of selecting, organizing, and teaching available information to make it more intelligible and more usable. In general, the recent studies shift the balance in learning from inventory to transaction. The structure of a discipline, its methods of inquiry, and the styles of thinking of its scholars and specialists offer important keys to this educational task.

Deciding What To Teach

Of the twelve areas of educational concern formulated earlier in this paper, seven focus attention on decisions about what to teach. Three are especially relevant to this conference because they concern priorities for the school, the school's role in dealing with national problems related to youth, and the selection of content.

ESTABLISHING PRIORITIES FOR THE SCHOOL

The question, "What shall the schools teach?" and its counterpart, "What shall the schools not teach?" constitutes a central issue in attempts to appraise American education. Stated in behavioral terms, the question is, "What should the graduate be able to do that he could not do if he had not gone to school?"

At a general level, there is agreement. Laymen and educators alike agree that the school has a major responsibility for preparing young people to live in today's society. They agree that the school has a responsibility for preparing young people to live with change and to contribute to constructive change. They agree that the school has a responsibility for helping the individual find and develop his own unique ways to personal satisfaction, recognizing that within the range of behavior that is acceptable to society there is room for much individual variation. At a more specific level, they agree that the student should read, write, speak, compute, and think more effectively than he would had he not gone to school.

Great differences of opinion appear, however, when educators and laymen, together or separately, approach the more complex tasks that come next. These are the tasks of (1) deciding the knowledge, skills, and values that are needed by children and young people; (2) determining which of these goals can best be achieved by the school and therefore should be included in the school program; (3) delineating the knowledge, skills, and values that can best be taught by the home, the church, and other social institutions; and (4) deciding which learnings require the joint efforts of the school and other agencies.

Thoughtful consideration of these questions is needed to determine priorities for the schools—to make sure, for example, that reading is identified as more important than cheerleading. Those responsible for deciding what to teach should apply concrete standards.

In the problem of what to teach, the value of any single item must be analyzed in terms of four criteria: desirability, attainability, feasibility, and clarity of meaning. In appraising the worth of a set of objectives as contrasted with a single goal, there are also four criteria: priority, comprehensiveness, balance, and consistency.

Decisions about the basic educational responsibilities of the school are essential for resolving the question of priorities. In determining what the school ought properly to provide, educators and the public may find it helpful to apply the following criteria: (1) Is it learning that is based substantially upon the arts and sciences? (2) Is it learning of complex and difficult things that require organization of experience and distribution of practice over long periods of time? (3) Is it learning in which the essential factors are not obvious to one observing the phenomenon and where the principles, concepts, and meanings must be brought specially to the attention of the learner? (4) Is it an experience that cannot be provided directly in the ordinary activities of daily living? (5) Is it learning that requires a more purified experience than is commonly available in life outside the school? (Schools should not be lifelike; they should be better than life.) (6) Is it learning that requires re-examination and interpretation of experience? [2]

The National Committee for the Project on Instruction made the following recommendation on priorities:

Priorities for the school are the teaching of skills in reading,

---

[2] Ralph W. Tyler, "Emphasize Tasks Appropriate for the School," *Phi Delta Kappan*, Vol. 40, No. 2 (November 1958), pp. 73–74.

composition, listening, speaking (both native and foreign languages), and computation . . . ways of creative and disciplined thinking, including methods of inquiry and application of knowledge . . . competence in self-instruction and independent learning . . . fundamental understanding of the humanities and the arts, the social sciences and natural sciences, and mathematics . . . appreciation of and discriminating taste in literature, music, and the visual arts . . . instruction in health education and physical education.

Responsibilities best met by joint efforts of the school and other social agencies include: development of values and ideals . . . social and civic competence . . . vocational preparation.

The decision to include or exclude particular school subjects or outside-of-class activities should be based on: (a) the priorities assigned to the school and to other agencies; (b) data about learners and society, and developments in the academic disciplines; (c) the human and material resources available in the school and community.[3]

YOUTH PROBLEMS AND THE SCHOOL

The school's role in dealing with national problems such as youth unemployment and juvenile delinquency is easy to define and difficult to enact. The role of the school is to provide a program that makes sense to the total school population, that challenges and persuades all children and youth to remain in school because something recognizably valuable is being provided. Fulfillment of this role is important for the young people themselves and vital to the survival of society.

A school staff that faces its instructional problems realistically will find much valuable help in the growing body of information about children and youth in today's society, particularly about urban children and youth. Current studies in sociology, psychology, and education yield information about factors that frequently deter learning and about ways in which schools can cope with these factors. The studies challenge some of the assumptions and point out some of the misconceptions that have stood in the way of educating children who are economically and culturally deprived.

One misconception has to do with the intellectual capacities of these young people. Much work has been done, and much more needs to be done, to devise techniques that provide accurate information about the intellectual and creative capacities of people from all kinds of backgrounds, and particularly those from economically and culturally deprived groups. Most of the commonly used standardized tests of intelligence and achievement

---

[3] *Schools for the Sixties,* a report of the NEA Project on Instruction (New York: McGraw-Hill Book Co., 1963), pp. 32–33.

are inappropriate for these young people, and the evidence they yield is not reliable.

Because inappropriate or unreliable measuring instruments are used, many children and youth from culturally disadvantaged backgrounds are unfairly labeled. As a result, they are misunderstood, mistaught, and misdirected. Their unrecognized intelligence is assaulted but not dented by an instructional program that has little relationship to their unique needs or their real potentials. Bored with the whole process of schooling, many young people mark time until the day they can remove themselves physically from the school they long ago deserted psychologically. To their credit, some of these misjudged youth stubbornly refuse to accept the label that is placed upon them. Too often, however, the label is just about what their earlier experiences have taught them to expect. It is accepted, and this acceptance in itself effectively blocks the effort to learn—sometimes permanently.

Another assumption is that a large number of children who are economically and culturally deprived—in particular, the potential dropouts—are not interested in education. This assumption rests heavily, but precariously, on the fact that many of these young people are discontented with school. They are discontented with school, but they are not necessarily disinterested in education. In their experience and in their vocabulary, "school" and "education" are not always synonymous.

Whatever their intelligence and rate of learning, the young people who drop out of school at an early age share one characteristic: a school record of difficulty and failure. The implication seems to be fairly obvious: potential dropouts must be identified. More important, the points at which the school is failing these young people and the reasons why it is failing them must be identified. Schools must exercise initiative in developing programs more likely to meet the needs of these students. They must explore the increasing number of experimental programs and try out the practices that seem most promising and most appropriate. There must be communication and work with community groups and organizations that are helping, or can help, with the solution of some of the problems.

So much attention has been given the school and community dropout problems of large cities that the need to strengthen rural schools has been overshadowed. Many of the school difficulties of rural migrants to these cities—Washington and Chicago, for example—have been aggravated by poor preparation. This is often, but not always, the result of segregation. Mountain areas of Kentucky and Tennessee need help for their schools, and President Johnson has called for special assistance in these areas.

The problems of the dropout, the unemployed youth, and the juvenile delinquent are serious ones for both the individual and society. But the attacks that are being made on the problems are vigorous and constructive and the results are encouraging. The following recommendation was made by the NEA Project on Instruction concerning this issue:

> The schools can help to combat such serious national problems as youth unemployment and juvenile delinquency by: (a) evaluating the intellectual and creative potential of *all* students; (b) identifying early the potential dropout and delinquent; (c) developing positive programs to challenge these young people to educational endeavor; (d) participating in cooperative programs with parents and with community groups and organizations—business and industry, labor, service groups, government agencies and the many youth-serving agencies.[4]

SELECTING CONTENT

The amount of knowledge from which to choose is overpowering in its magnitude, and the rate at which advances are being made is so rapid that new developments arise before old ones are fully understood. Never before have the dynamic forces of change worked with such incredible speed. In the nearly 2,000 years since the birth of Christ, there has been first a very slow and then a rapidly accelerating growth in the accumulation of knowledge. If this accumulation is plotted on a time line, beginning with the birth of Christ, the first doubling of knowledge occurs in 1750; the second in 1900; the third in 1950; and the fourth only ten years later, in 1960!

So much has been learned in so many areas of knowledge that it is no longer possible for students to learn even summaries of existing knowledge. Sheer bulk defeats any effort to teach knowledge as a body of facts to be learned. Furthermore, a radical reorganization of a given body of knowledge can be expected not once in the remainder of this century but several times. The school problem once known as "coverage" is now meaningless and obsolete. Coverage is no longer difficult; it is impossible.

The problems of what to learn and how to learn it require a different approach today. Students need ways to move from memorization of facts to discovery of facts; they need ways to learn to think as physicists think, as historians think, as artists think. One scholar puts it this way: the problem is one of moving from a rhetoric of conclusions to an experience in inquiry.

[4] *Ibid.*, p. 37.

How, then, can schools make wise selections of content? How can they make intelligent use of the findings and methods of the disciplines? And, in the process, what are the appropriate roles of academic scholars, educators, and laymen? The National Committee for the Project on Instruction makes three recommendations:

1. The objectives of the school, with a clear statement of priorities, should give direction to all curriculum planning. This applies to adding content, eliminating content, or changing the emphases on various topics and fields of study.

2. Each curriculum area should be under continuous study and evaluation and should be reviewed periodically. One purpose of such reviews is to determine whether recent findings in the academic disciplines are, or should be, reflected in the instructional program. These reviews should utilize the knowledge and skills of the teacher, the school administrator, the scholar in the academic disciplines, the scholar in the profession of teaching, and the informed lay citizen, with each contributing his special competence to the total task.

3. In selecting content, school staffs should study the results and recommendations of curriculum projects sponsored by nationally oriented groups with a view to applying promising findings.

There should be a systematic procedure for studying the results of these curriculum projects. The procedure should recognize the importance of balance and continuity in the total school experience of students and include the steps prerequisite to curriculum changes.[5]

Organizing the School and the Classroom

The tasks of planning and organizing for teaching are complex and demanding. This is a fact, but its truth is not always recognized, even by some members of the teaching profession. From those who do not recognize the complexity of the tasks come superficial approaches and naïve proposals. From those who recognize both the difficulty and the importance of the tasks must come careful study, creative proposals, and promising innovations. Current educational innovations can be classified as follows: (1) practices directed to fuller and more effective utilization of human talent; (2) practices directed to fuller and more effective utilization of time; and (3) practices directed to a fuller and more effective utilization of technology.[6]

---

5 *Ibid.,* pp. 50, 51, 55.
6 Lester W. Nelson, "A Perspective on Innovation in Education." An unpublished paper delivered at a National Education Association staff meeting, Washington, D.C., October 31, 1962.

The National Committee for the Project on Instruction has made several recommendations concerning school and classroom organization. The following are two examples:

1. The vertical organization of the school should provide for the continuous, unbroken, upward progression of all learners, with due recognition of the wide variability among learners in every aspect of their development. The school organization should, therefore, provide for differentiated rates and means of progression toward achievement of educational goals.

Nongrading and multi-grading are promising alternatives to the traditional graded school and should be given careful consideration in seeking to provide flexible progress plans geared to human variability.

2. In order to provide individually planned programs for learners, taking into account the specific objectives to be achieved, the horizontal organization of the school should permit flexibility in assigning pupils to instructional groups that may range in size from one pupil to as many as a hundred or more. Well-planned co-operative efforts among teachers—efforts such as team teaching, for example—should be encouraged and tested.[7]

Education cannot muddle through in the traditional setting in the traditional way while the rest of society promptly employs new technical resources and reorganizes whole industries on the basis of their use. Fortunately, the press for efficiency, variety, and aesthetics in school design and for the use of technology at appropriate points in the school program is well begun.

In both new and old buildings, technological developments such as television, tape recordings, teaching machines, language laboratories, and films and filmstrips already have made marked contributions to the curriculum. Their use is expected to spread widely in the future. Computers have been tried in the complicated task of developing a master schedule, where pupils' and teachers' time, course offerings, and classroom space somehow have to be matched. A number of schools have already been built that architecturally reflect the best current knowledge about learning and aids to learning. The designs stress flexibility and amenity in the school environment. The tremendous potential of new instructional materials and technology has also been recognized in the committee's recommendations on the use of educational television and radio, programmed learning, instructional materials centers, and automation.

---

[7] *Schools for the Sixties,* a report of the NEA Project on Instruction (McGraw-Hill Book Co., 1963), p. 78.

Evaluation of Students

There is a growing body of literature questioning some of the current ways of evaluating student progress and potential, so that a study of this subject is now not only at a turning point but is more than ever full of controversy. There is no point to testing students for a catalog of their knowledge in a given discipline if educators are agreed that the disciplines ought to be taught in terms of principles and appropriate methods of inquiry. Students will then be evaluated on their ability to recognize and apply to fresh data the principles and methods they have discovered. It is essential that new instruments of evaluation be developed in order to adequately measure progress in identifying and using such principles and methods.

For many years, the concept of most people (professional educators and psychologists included) of the human mind and its functioning was largely limited by the concepts embodied in intelligence tests. Though presumably no developer of intelligence tests meant to imply that an intelligence test assessed all of man's intellectual functioning, educators have often behaved as though this were so. It has almost always been the sole instrument used in assessing intellectual potential, mental growth, and the like; and it has been heavily relied upon to determine who was mentally retarded and gifted. Unfortunately, such tests have usually shaped the educational curricula and methods to bring about the kind of growth or achievement that is related to the mental abilities involved in intelligence or scholastic aptitude tests. Measures of educational achievement have also been patterned along these same lines.

Although there are a number of lines of research that have contributed to an expanded concept of the human mind from the old narrow definition of intelligence that "intelligence is what intelligence tests measure," the efforts related to creative thinking abilities have done much to push this expanded concept into the consciousness of educators. This research points to some of the things that must be done to bring about a higher level of mental health and educational achievement.

Education is not more humane because it has failed to recognize differences among children in their ways of learning. Some tend to learn by authority and are anxious to please their teacher—these will respond favorably if the teacher rewards correct responses. Some children, on the other hand, tend to learn spontaneously or creatively—by exploring, testing the limits, searching, inquiring, manipulating, and even playing. It appears that research on the relationship between mental abilities and procedures of instruction, an area which has never really been explored, might be truly promising and may lead to an understanding of what it really means to individualize instruction.

A broader concept of the human mind and its functioning opens up many new and exciting possibilities. It places new emphasis on what man may become. It suggests that the vast army of dropouts can be educated to a higher degree than was previously thought possible. There is already evidence of "hopeless" individuals who began to learn successfully when permitted to learn creatively rather than by authority and when they were rewarded for this kind of achievement. Drastic changes in evaluation techniques will accompany changes in instruction. As it becomes apparent that most of life's questions do not have one correct answer but numerous alternatives, the old model of test construction will fall.[8]

Mission of Teacher Education

The foregoing recommendations for action to improve the nation's schools imply some knowledge and action by the teacher at every point—in many instances, knowledge and action that are now the exception rather than the rule. The education of teachers is going through a slow metamorphosis and the recommendations of the Conant report and other reforms proposed by educational leaders are by now familiar.[9]

Admittedly, the implications of the recommendations for an improved curriculum present a tall order for any teacher. Teachers themselves are no less affected by changes in our society than are their pupils; and their preparation in the disciplines can be outdated by expanded knowledge just as rapidly. Comfortable and apparently successful teaching habits can be threatened by new theories of learning. For aspiring and fledgling teachers, all of these pressures can confuse and impede a good start in the field.

In general, two factors are paramount in professional education today: increased breadth of liberal education and an emphasis upon flexibility. All education for all professions—teaching, social work, law, and the like—should be on the graduate level. Undergraduates in teacher education, nursing, and so on, should be curtailed and eliminated as rapidly as possible. First, of

[8] Dr. Robert D. Strom, Assistant Director, NEA School Dropouts Project, has studied trends in evaluation, and he has permitted the writer to draw on one of his unpublished papers for this section. *See* Robert D. Strom, "Midnight Evaluations of Evaluation." Unpublished paper, Washington, D.C., 1963.

[9] James B. Conant, *The Education of American Teachers* (New York: McGraw-Hill Book Co., 1963).

course, the liberal arts programs must be overhauled so that the student entering the professional graduate school of education or social work is liberally educated. At the moment, most liberal arts programs are neither "liberal" nor "art."

Communication among the disciplines and the professions is difficult at best. For the future professional workers, teachers and social workers, to be sealed off even slightly by undergraduate specialization in professional courses rather than content courses is to limit opportunity for study in depth in a discipline and for exploration of other fields of knowledge. Moreover, it encourages a wider separation later, when a continuing pursuit of general education plus refreshment in one's own content field is of the highest priority.

In discussing what constitutes general education, the general requirements for the bachelor's degree in a program of teacher education, and the assumptions on which such requirements rests, Dr. Conant states:

> . . . the assumptions are neither new nor far to seek. They are: first, that there are certain areas of knowledge with which all future teachers should be acquainted; second, that in these areas of knowledge there are characteristic ways of grasping the subject; third, that in both the knowledge and the ways of understanding them there are basic principles; finally, that properly studied and taught, these subjects and the principles discoverable in them can further the process of a liberal education. . . . If the teachers in a school system are to be a group of learned persons cooperating together, they should have as much intellectual experience in common as possible, and any teacher who has not studied in a variety of fields in college will always feel far out of his depth . . . in a field other than his own.[10]

Conant recommends that teachers be educated in four years rather than five. But if students are taught to think as physicists think and as historians think, it follows no less in the education of their teachers. It also follows that the least one can expect of a teacher is to know the general frontiers of a discipline. The following remarks, prepared for the NEA Project on Instruction, are as true for teachers as for laymen:

> The layman needs to know where the growth points of a discipline are located (and why they are growth points) because ignorance of them will mean that what he learned about a discipline in his schooling will otherwise collapse around his ears.

---

10 Conant, *op. cit.*, pp. 92–93.

. . . Because the layman is the ultimate user of knowledge, the man who must act and undergo, he needs a view of the discipline from another vantage point. For actors and undergoers are better as they know what they are doing and why. Blind obedience to a routine, unquestioning obeisance to authoritative instruction produces inflexible actors and supine undergoers, neither of which are adequate to the rate of change which our technology and our ways of living now demand. The layman as giver of assent and cash support must see the disciplines from still a third angle. He must understand something of the sweat, patience, ingenuity, and insights which go into their making. He must understand something of their immediately material value to his pleasure and comfort. Otherwise he will not give his assent and his cash. Enquiry will languish, hence the resources of technology will not be replenished; thus our ability to solve our continuing stream of problems will fail. Finally, the layman, as a possible member of a discipline, needs a view of the discipline from still a fourth point of view. He needs to see, first, the kinds of skills and opportunities for individual action which each affords and rewards. Second, at some point, he needs a glimpse of the unsolved problems to which he, as a possible member, might contribute.[11]

It may be that breadth of education will also answer the imperative of flexibility. Certainly, the ability to entertain ideas related to many areas of learning and to view situations from more than one vantage point is, it is hoped, a by-product of a liberal education. This kind of flexibility can be bred out of students in their professional education, however, if that portion of their experience narrows down to "a one true way" to approach problems to be solved in their own field.

It is perhaps too much to expect that the prevailing school of thought in a given institution or under a particular mentor will not have its impact on students; it is, however, doing them a disservice to turn out pale carbon copies who do not have the ability or flexibility to strike out in other directions later in their professional lives. This does not mean that a professional curriculum must be a bland catch-all. It does mean that flexibility cannot be fostered in students if educators themselves cling to their pet theories in the face of new discoveries and changing times.

This paper has attempted to deal with a number of areas of concern to all educators by identifying issues and trends in school

---

[11] Joseph J. Schwab, "Education and the Structure of the Disciplines." Unpublished working paper prepared for the NEA Project on Instruction, Washington, D.C., 1961.

curriculum and organization and relating the implications of activities at this level to higher education, specifically to the training of teachers.

The issues taken up here have been discussed in terms of data about society, about the individual learner, and about organized knowledge. The purposes of education—a good education—were defined in terms of the individual rather than the national interest, although the implication intended was that the well-educated person, functioning effectively in his environment and having reached his own greatest potential, contributes most constructively to the society in which he lives. The function of the teacher, as expressed here, is to guide the learner toward discoveries and new experiences through which his behavior is changed and modified.

Of the issues brought up in this paper, the most crucial to a discussion of the purposes of the teaching profession as a whole is the question of establishment of priorities. Many of the aims of society depend more and more upon the education of its members. But this does not mean that all of the aims of society can be met by those in education. It is of paramount importance, therefore, that everyone, but most particularly teachers at all levels, identify the great social issues and explore these issues as they relate to education, rather than to concentrate on the problems that arise out of these issues.

The issues of poverty and discrimination relate to the use of the schools as an instrument of social change, out of which a whole host of problems has arisen. The position of the United States, internally and in world affairs, has contributed increasingly to the use of universities as a research arm of the federal government, a situation that has important implications for the teaching profession.

Where does the intellectual development of young people fit in this complex? This fundamental purpose of the teaching profession can be distorted and lost without constant redefinition. It is the first responsibility of the profession.

3

EDUCATION OF
SOCIAL WORKERS

By Ruth E. Smalley

Social workers, and their predecessors who were moved by the same compassions and interests that today lead to the choice of this profession, are concerned with people as whole human beings, in relationship to other people and within the context, structures and institutional forms of a society. Their specific concern is with the flowering of the human spirit. Albert Schweitzer puts it in other words: "Judging by what I have learned about men and women I am convinced that there is far more in them of idealist will power than ever comes to the surface of the world . . . to unbind what is bound, to bring the underground waters to the surface: mankind is waiting and longing for such as can do that."

Social work's effort is directed toward unbinding what is bound and bringing the underground waters to the surface. It seeks to release human power and psychological power for the attainment of social good. The achievement of social work's goal marks the coming together of an individual's realization of himself as an individual who is social, and society's realization of itself as the kind of society that supports and furthers such self-realization for all individuals.

Social work then is concerned both with the nature of social conditions as they interfere with or further the release of human power for social good, and with the direct and immediate releasing of that power individual by individual, group by group, or community by community, within the purpose of some specific social agency or institution created by society in its own interest and in the interest of individuals and groups of individuals within it.

Social work is an institutionalized profession. Its purposes are mainly discharged not by private practitioners but by social workers employed within social agencies, established by society as a whole or some substantial segment of it, to deal with characteristic problems which considerable numbers of people face, and to provide services they can use toward the release of their human power for social good.

That is what social work is trying to do: to release human power for the achievement of social good, and to release social power for the creation of the kind of society that makes social self-realization most possible.

In defining its purpose as a professional membership organization the National Association of Social Workers by implication defines the purposes of the whole profession.

> To promote the quality and effectiveness of social work practice in the United States of America through services to the individual, the group, and the community;
>
> To further the broad objective of improving conditions of life in our democratic society through utilization of the professional knowledge and skills of social work, and to expand through research the knowledge necessary to define and attain these goals;
>
> To provide opportunity for the social work profession to work in unity toward maintaining and promoting high standards of practice and of preparation for practice and toward alleviating or preventing sources of deprivation, distress and strain susceptible of being influenced by social work methods and by social action.[1]

Social workers are a form of action concerned with formulating social policy, effecting social legislation, administering a program of services as executive or subexecutive, or getting a particular social service to a clientele at the direct service level, as social caseworker, social group worker, or community organization worker. Their action involves the use of a relationship skill directed toward a social purpose, whatever the specific social work process engaged in, and whatever the field of practice within which it is used.

The major social work processes have been identified as social casework, social group work, community organization (the primary processes that reach the clientele directly), and supervision, administration, research, and teaching (of social work), sometimes called secondary or facilitating processes. Supervision, administration, research and teaching in social work are recognized as having elements in common with those processes in other professions and disciplines. But when they are used toward social work ends by social workers, within social agencies or institutions that have social sanction for their practice, and when they include in addition to the use of knowledge and skill shared with other groups and professions, the use of social work knowledge and social work skill, they may be considered to fall under the heading of social work practice. Students

---

[1] *Bylaws of the National Association of Social Workers* (New York: National Association of Social Workers, 1963).

in schools of social work are specifically prepared to engage in them, at the post-master's level, but within the context of their professional education as social workers.

Major fields of practice for social work in all of its processes both primary and secondary, are generally recognized as family counseling; public assistance agencies; child welfare agencies, including child placement and adoption services, protective services and services to children in their own homes; correctional institutions; educational institutions; medical clinics and hospitals; psychiatric clinics and hospitals; programs of residential care; group- and neighborhood-serving agencies; and community planning and co-ordinating agencies.

When a social worker engages in social action, he does so either as an employee of a social agency, as a member of the professional membership organization, or as a private citizen. As an employee of a social agency, or as a member of his professional organization, he is bound by the values, purpose, and ethics of his profession and constrained to use the knowledge and skill that are distinctively his as a professional social worker. When he acts as a private citizen it is hoped that he would be a sufficiently integrated personality so that his action would not do violence to the values and skill that are his as a social worker.

The requirement of using a relationship skill toward social purpose, wherever and whenever social work practice is applied, is crucial to the content and nature of social work education.

The common objective that unites social work and education is the creation of a better world by enabling people to live within it and participate in shaping it, or by "releasing individual and social power for social good." Social workers seek to accomplish that purpose primarily by developing and administering programs of social services, and by getting those services to the clientele for whom they are designed in a way that makes them most usable and most truly in the interest of individual and social welfare. In the course of such activity and as members of an organized profession and of a variety of social welfare organizations they also influence and formulate social policy and social legislation. There is no prescribed curriculum of social services that all persons must use. Rather they have been developed on the basis of individual and group needs or problems and they are offered and used when need or problem coincides with social agency purpose and program. They are society-financed, whether by tax funds or voluntary contribution, in society's own interest, as well as in the interest of the individuals and groups served. As individuals and groups are well served through adequate programs of skillfully administered social service, power for individually fulfilled and socially constructive living is released.

Primary and secondary education on the other hand seeks primarily to develop and release in all children and youth intellectual power—power to use the skills that comprise literacy, as well as those specific communications and vocational skills, and a body of knowledge about man and society for informed, intelligent, productive participation in society. To this end a prescribed program of education is required of all children and youth (with allowance for individual choice particularly toward the upper end). This program seeks to develop skills in reading, writing, figuring, and communicating; it seeks to pass on a body of knowledge about man and his world, and to develop an appreciation of the way men have responded over the ages to their world. It is because this kind of knowledge and skill and appreciation is recognized as essential for all citizens in a democracy, if a democracy is going to work, that the program is both prescribed in its broad limits and universally required.

All educators would probably agree that the educational program should be made available through a living school experience, which is conducive not only to every child's learning what his society says he should and what his society hopes he will learn, but which is conducive as well to his developing, within the social situation of "school," his capacities for a constructive and individually fulfilled life. It is this kind of living experience that will help make possible the use of his education toward socially desirable ends.

Nature of Social Work Education

Educational programs designed to train future social workers who embody social work values, and who are prepared through knowledge and skill to achieve social work ends, have certain common identifiable characteristics. Such a program may be viewed as a process, an experience characterized by duration in time, which has a beginning, a middle and an end.[2]

The entire program is designed to release in the students the power to become social workers. There is something in the nature of the educational experience itself, in its engagement of the student to use the school for his own chosen ends, that is similar to the very process he will be using as a social worker. For he will be seeking to engage individuals, groups and communities in using social work services or programs for their chosen ends, even though, as in certain protective or school social work services, the original initiative, or decision for intervention comes from the outside, and may not be the client's own until he is helped to make it his own.

---

[2] The program leading to the basic professional degree, master of social work, covers two academic years of full-time study in class and field.

There are psychological principles that govern the way an individual can be helped to find a goal and work toward it with increasing commitment to the use of his own powers, and these principles are as true for a program of social work education as for a program of social work. As the student engages in an educational experience that helps him to become a social worker, through his relationship with teachers, supervisors, and classmates, as well as through his acquisition of knowledge, he gains the ability to engage in the same kind of psychological relationship process with individual clients, groups, or communities seeking to use the services he is making available.

This kind of educational experience is further characterized by its embodying a program of class and field work, within which a defined body of knowledge is transmitted, and professional skill in its use developed. It is field work, so central a part of all social work education, that provides the opportunity for the student to learn through doing, and to both test and develop further what he knows and can do.

The program is characterized by a sequence in all of its aspects and areas, with educational experiences building on what has gone before and leading on to what is to follow. It is characterized by provision for an integration of all of its parts, facilitated by educational structures and processes, but occurring within the student as he puts himself to work as a thinking, feeling, and acting social worker.

Admissions Process

Schools of social work seek to select students who at this point of admission already have the basic values, knowledge, intellectual ability and maturity that make it possible for them to become social workers within a two-year educational period. Nothing short of graduation from a liberal arts college with a good record of intellectual achievement, and with a record of participation in activities that reflect an interest in and capacity to work with people, can suffice to give schools some assurance that they are getting the human material required. Further assurance is gained from the admissions process itself with its required letters of reference, transcript of undergraduate record, health examination form, written statement of purpose in applying to a school of social work, and most of all its personal interview through which an applicant and his (faculty member) interviewer seek to know whether he is right for education for social work, and whether education for social work is right for him.

Sequences in undergraduate programs have been developed

throughout the country, fostered, encouraged, and guided by the Council on Social Work Education itself. These programs are designed with three goals in mind: (1) to prepare for immediate entry into nonprofessional social welfare positions; (2) to provide a valuable preparation for learning in the graduate schools of social work; and (3) to serve as an undergraduate major in a liberal arts program leading to effective and informed citizen participation in community life. While such a sequence is not required by any professional school of social work for entrance, and while it has not been demonstrated that it is necessarily the best or only way for all students to prepare for professional education, it is making increasingly important contributions through the achievement of all of its three objectives.

The admissions process in a school of social work not only helps schools select the right students, but it helps the student select a school and commit himself more firmly and more knowledgeably, in the course of the admissions process itself, to an experience in social work education, looking toward a career in social work.

Once the student is enrolled he follows, in the main, a required curriculum, although most schools of social work make provision for some electives in accordance with a student's special interest. Required courses fall into three sequences: social welfare policy and services; human behavior and the social environment; and methods of social work practice. These three content areas reflect the educational objectives of preparing students for a profession that is concerned with the restoration, maintenance, and enhancement of the social functioning of individuals and groups through practice within social agencies or institutions designed to accomplish the same purposes. To achieve such a purpose the student must come to understand (1) the kinds of institutional provisions made in the past and present in this country and abroad to further the social functioning of individuals, groups and communities; (2) the way individuals, groups, and communities grow and change, what furthers or interferes with healthy growth in the individual, and how problems in and deviations from healthy growth and social functioning may be expressed; (3) the methods of administering social services and getting social agency services to individuals, groups, and communities through a human relationships skill; and (4) some principles of scientific inquiry or research basic to participation in improving social work practice and social welfare programs.

Social Welfare Policy and Services

Content in this sequence is covered through a series of courses within a conceptual framework that has been identified as appropriate for and required in all professional schools of social work. The sequence includes the following objectives for the student:

1. To understand the nature of human need and its causation as the product of the social, political, and economic configuration of society, which also shapes the social work institutions designed to meet the need.

2. To grasp the impact of change on human needs and social work structure and functions, historically and in the present, in his own and in other societies.

3. To understand the nature of social welfare organizations, public and private, at the local, state, and federal levels; the role of government in its changing responsibility to promote the general welfare; the heritage of his society and the social work profession; and to build his own code of ethics and values for a responsible use of himself in his professional activities.

4. To understand the nature of "agency" (and its impact on the client) as a community-sanctioned, organized effort, and to find his proper place and responsibility within it and within the community.

In relation to the total curriculum this sequence can be likened to a map of the real terrain of society, its culture and institutions, within which the person served, the community, and the profession act and react, and within which social problems are generated and social work programs are created. It furnishes the student with the realities of the milieu within which he and the person served work out the goal of re-establishing the desired equilibrium of the individual and society. Expectation is placed on the student that he be responsible for knowledge and understanding of the content in this sequence as indivisible from his social work practice and as complementary to his learning in the other curriculum sequences.

Content for the courses that make up this sequence is drawn largely from the social work profession's own knowledge. However, content from related disciplines such as economics, political science, anthropology, and sociology is used as well, and is taught in its relation to social work knowledge. The aim is to develop an understanding needed by social workers of the social welfare milieu within which they will function.

A further objective of this sequence is to help the student appreciate the meaning of working as a member of an institutionalized profession, of functioning within and as an integral part of a social agency, using his professional relationship skill to help the agency accomplish its purpose as an agency, which is also one manifestation of his purpose as a professional social worker, in a way that makes for the fulfillment and growth of the individuals, groups and communities served, and is conducive to the welfare of society as a whole.

Such an objective requires his learning to participate responsibly and appropriately in the growth and change of the agency of which he is a part, and in the growth and change of the pattern of social agency services locally and more broadly.

Human Behavior and the Social Environment

Content in this sequence is covered through a series of courses offered over the four terms of the master's degree program within a frame of reference relevant for the purposes of social work. The objectives of the sequence for the student are:

1. To develop in the student a sense of values about people, to revere and respect human life, to understand the nature of human strivings and the ways in which human beings seek to fulfill themselves as social beings.

2. To comprehend a psychology of process central to which is the affirmation of man's unity, his purposefulness, and his ability to make choices, not only on the basis of past determination, but in terms of the processes going on currently, both within himself and in the outer world of human relationships. Since man is seen in continuing and changing interaction with other men, and with the material world, a psychology of process is relativistic, considers the concomitant presence of opposing processes, takes into account the unpredictable and uncertain in man's nature, and leaves room for the spontaneous and unique occurrences in growth and development.

3. To understand the nature of stress and the range of normal and deviant behavior or dysfunction in its physical, psychological, and social manifestations; to understand individual difference as related to genetic endowment and to life experience, the environment and the culture.

4. To comprehend the social environment as providing the potential for human development, and as being contributive to the growth of individuals and groups at the same time that it sets or represents limits.

5. To release his own creative human power as a helper disciplined for use on behalf of the other person.

This sequence provides the biological and psychological foundations underlying the practice theory taught in the methods of practice course and in field work. It includes courses dealing with the nature of physical and mental illness in their relation to health. Physicians, psychiatrists, and psychologists are commonly used in conjunction with social work faculty to teach the illness or dysfunction aspects of this sequence.

The life cycle is taught, within this sequence, in its chronological development from conception through old age. Periods of crisis and stress are identified as offering opportunity for growth and the development of new resources, as well as constituting hazard (e.g., birth, weaning, training relating to both parents and to siblings, school, adolescence, choosing and getting started on a vocation, marrying, parenthood, late maturity, problems of declining strength and increased responsibilities, and old age).

Emphasized in the objectives of this sequence is the teaching of a psychology of human growth, which sees the individual as the center of his own life, growing within relationships, acting upon and creating his environment as well as being acted upon. References from the fields of embryology, biology, anthropology, education, psychology, philosophy, psychiatry, and psychoanalysis support such a position. Such references, and carefully selected fiction and biography as well, can be used to develop a psychological base for helping that utilizes and furthers what the individual group or community has within itself of power for growth, or of "idealist will power." The teaching of this sequence involves as well the student's becoming aware of himself, his own motivations, blind spots, biases and human resources. It furthers his use of the sequence and the entire educational experience for personal growth. Such growth leads to a sensitive, compassionate, generous use of his scientific knowledge in all of his professional relationships.

Methods of Social Work Practice

Content in this sequence is covered through a sequence of courses in the method that constitutes the student's method or process of concentration. In the master's program, students elect a concentration in social casework, social group work, or community organization. There are theoretical formulations for casework and for group work, and a beginning theoretical formulation for community organization as methods that are taught as practice theory, and as revealed in recorded practice material—both the student's own, and what is introduced by the instructor. The choice of method concentration determines whether an individual student's sequence of methods courses and his field work placement will be in social casework, social group work, or community organization. While there is some difference in the theoretical formulations of practice method taught as between school and school, particularly in respect to casework, such formulations are ordinarily consistent within a given school so that the student may develop a reliable operating base for his practice. Furthermore, there is sufficient likeness in theoretical base for practice among all schools so that mobility of graduates is assured, with differences constituting a potential enrichment to the field as a whole.

There are certain principles that govern all processes in social work, both the basic or primary processes of casework, social group work, and community organization, and the secondary or facilitating processes of supervision, administration, research, and education for social work. But it is important to teach those principles *distinctive* to each of the above processes, as well as common to them. A conception of the significance of the employing social agency's purpose and function should also be emphasized to give content and direction to social work processes, thus assuring social accountability.

Teaching method in this sequence, as in most courses in the curriculum, involves discussion in groups of twenty-five or fewer students to facilitate the active engagement of each student in the learning experience, in interaction with the other students and with the instructor. Use of the student's own case or group record material in practice or methods classes, drawn from his current or recent experience in the field, help him to identify principles of practice as they are reflected in (or missing from) his own and his classmates' work and aids his learning principles of practice and their use.

It is recognized that all social workers, whatever the process they use most consistently (social casework, social group work, community organization), work with individuals, groups, and communities. For this reason schools of social work have developed various methods for helping all students understand the similarities and differences of the three processes, and even, in some instances, to have some planned experience in a process or processes other than the one of concentration.

While the concentration in the master's degree program is by method or process skill (casework, group work, community organization) rather than by field of practice (family counseling, school social work, and so on) it is possible for a student to gain, within the "generic curriculum" described, special knowledge of a field of practice, as well as special skill in a social work process.[3] This may be achieved through placement in a specific field (family counseling, school social work, corrections); through special elective courses or seminars focused on the particular field of practice; through the research project's use of data from the field of practice which constitutes the field work placement; as well as through enrichment of the total curriculum with content drawn from the specific practice field.

Administration

The curriculum as a whole, as well as the methods sequence, is designed to include, as appropriate to the pattern of the individual school, content that helps the student learn to function as a member of a social agency staff with appreciation of his place in the adminis-

---

[3] All social work processes, both primary and secondary, can be used within any field of practice.

trative organization, and in a way that is contributive to the total agency operation.

Research

Out of an appreciation of the significance of all students' under-standing the importance of research to social work's contribution as a profession, every student is required to learn basic principles of scientific inquiry and to employ them in a research project, either singly or as a member of a group of students. Even more important is the development of the "research attitude" that should permeate every student's professional activity—an attitude of questioning, seeking additional knowledge, trying to find a better way—even as he develops enough conviction about what he presently knows to be able to operate from it with confidence and sureness.

Doctoral Programs

Doctoral programs, increasingly available in schools of social work, seek to develop scholarly and professional competence at an advanced level, and to prepare students for responsible and creative leadership in the field, ordinarily though not exclusively through research, ad-ministration, or teaching. They include advanced social work con-tent, and knowledge of other disciplines, primarily the social and behavioral sciences as they are related to social work, and they re-quire demonstration of scholarship through the preparation of a dissertation.

Field Work

The place of field work in the curriculum of all schools of social work is central. This is true for both historical and educational reasons. The earliest schools of social work were developed as in-service train-ing programs within social agencies, as agencies' ways of preparing staff to work more helpfully and effectively. With the incorporation of schools of social work within universities, and with the initiation of schools within universities as is currently required, curricula have gained in depth and breadth of knowledge, but they have never lost the vitality and reality assured by the field experience which con-tinues to hold its focal place in the total educational program.

Currently, every student is required to be placed for field work in a social agency in both years of the master's degree program. Here he is actively engaged in developing and using a relationship skill in making some agency service available to the recipients of some social work service. Here he is constrained to use what he knows and is learning in class and field, in service that is increasingly helpful and responsible. Here he discovers what he does not know or cannot do that he must make his own if he is to accomplish his own purpose of becoming a social worker. So it is that each student both learns in the classroom and experiences in the field what social work is; and what it requires of internalized values, available knowledge, and operative helping skill.

Several factors combine to further field work's being an integral part of a total educational program. Field work agencies are selected according to criteria defined by each school to assure their suitability for student learning, and through a process that attests to the willingness and desire of the agency to be part of the student's learning experience. The field supervisors, too, are selected according to defined criteria that assure practice and supervisory interest and competence. The student keeps detailed written records of his part and the part of the client or group in what goes on between them, and submits his records to his supervisor prior to a regular weekly conference of one to two hours duration. In these conferences with his field work supervisor, his records are used as the primary source of his learning. Conferences focus on how the student is using his knowledge and himself to give the agency's service in a compassionate, helpful, and responsible way. Principles of practice as they are evident in what the student has done, or as they are not evident but should have been, are identified and taught by the supervisor. The supervisor's focus is always on the student, and on how he is functioning in all the ways required of a social worker engaged in giving a particular agency service. "How he is functioning" must be related to where he is in the time span of the two years of professional education: where and how he is effective, where and how he is not; where he is not what seems to be responsible; lack of knowledge in some content areas; a problem in relationship; a struggle with values he is expected to embody or with agency policy he is expected to represent. The supervisor's skill is directed toward helping the student move through the two years and meet requirements established by the school for field performance at the end of each of the four semesters. It is in the field that knowledge from all areas in the curriculum comes together for the student's integration and use. Here he is stimulated to return to classes and acquire new knowledge to carry his field work responsibilities.

Increasingly supervisors are making available, in a planned way, opportunities for learning in addition to the primary one for developing skill in the social work method that constitutes the student's concentration. For example, attention is given to how the student is using or failing to use what he is learning about administration, in the way he carries his administrative responsibilities in the agency and shows respect and consideration for others in the administrative organization, and for the procedures necessary for effective agency operation. He is given opportunity to develop and use his knowledge of community and community resources in a way appropriate to his placement as a student in the agency. He is helped to make the connection between broad-scale social policies and the program and operation of his own and other agencies— their services, resources, and organization. He may be offered an opportunity to use social work processes other than the one that constitutes his concentration, or to use some principles or processes other than those of his own process.

Continuous relation of the student supervisor to the school of social work through some faculty member designated to carry school-agency responsibility for a particular student, and through group meetings of supervisors called by the school assures the field's being educationally focused and integrated within a total learning experience. At the same time the field retains its important difference from the classroom by virtue of the realistic situation in which the student is placed, requiring action as a social worker.

While most schools now refer to field work as field instruction and to the field work supervisor as field instructor, in order to emphasize the educational purpose and nature of the field work experience as against an apprenticeship, the older terms are used here. There is a danger of making field work too didactic an experience, and so of failing to capitalize on its real-life quality, on the importance of the agency requirement for responsible service, which the student must meet, and on the significance of the relationship between supervisor and student as the medium through which learning takes place.

Integration of Learning

Most important in achieving integration of learning is a faculty's concept of the purpose of the profession for which they are preparing students, and so of the purpose of the educational program in which they are engaged. Then it is possible to see how the program's several parts, sequences, and experiences are related to each other toward the achievement of a single purpose. Such accord and affirmation of purpose not only determine content, but educational method, and suggests as well the kinds of structures and devices that can sustain and forward the educational process as a whole toward the achievement of educational purpose. In other words, it is the integration and wholeness of each faculty member, his grasp of and respect for the whole purpose of his school, and for his own and every other faculty and staff person's contribution to it, that makes it possible for each student to achieve integration in his learning. There follow such devices as the appointment of an adviser for every student, whose responsibility is to keep related to his advisee's field supervisor as well as to his other teachers in order that conferences may be used by the advisee to identify and work on learning problems as they occur.

It is possible also to hold regularly scheduled faculty meetings of all first-year and of all second-year teachers to consider how the several contents taught are related and how a given class of students is moving through the year, using or failing to use all parts of the educational experience. Chairmen of sequences may hold meetings of all faculty teaching in the sequence to assure progression, as well as integration in learning.

Regular planned meetings with field work supervisors and with agency executives, in small enough groups to make engagement fruitful, are commonly used as a method for integrating class and field work. The use in class of some of the student's recorded work or experience in the field is an additional way of furthering class and field integration. Use of data in the student's field work agency as the base for his research project, and use of his recorded practice in the development of a substantial paper on practice and on the theory underlying it, are still further ways of keeping class and field related. Concepts themselves can be unifying, when grasped by faculty and communicated to students for their use. As an illustration, one such concept as developed by Erik Erikson can be presented.[4] It relates to principles of child development and the importance of the kind of growth that provides opportunity for realization of the world into which the child goes when he reaches out from the immediate family circle. Erikson refers to the importance of the child's *trust* developing first (through his early relationship to the mother), then a sense of *autonomy* (i.e., a sense that he is a separate person and can operate as a separate person related to others), and finally a capacity for *reaching out,* for *initiative,* a capacity to do and to innovate, to go beyond what he can presently manage. Children may learn these lessons well, but if they find a world where their trust is too constantly betrayed, their opportunities for self-reliance and independent judgment severely limited, and their chance for using initiative minimal, they will indeed suffer frustration and fail to realize themselves as the socially contributive individuals they have been "trained" to be.

This is a unifying, integrative concept of growth and its requirements that directs social workers and teachers to help create the kind of environment, whether social agency, public school, school of social work, or the larger world where trust, autonomy, and

---

[4] Erik H. Erikson, "Identity and the Life Cycle," *Psychological Issues* (entire issue), Vol. 1, No. 1 (January 1959).

initiative are viable. It provides a frame of reference, within which schools of social work can ask of their programs: Does it build on and further a sense of trust in the student, provide the base for using his autonomy and his initiative as realistic and appropriate for him in this situation?

Ending Process in Social Work Education

A program of education for social work has been viewed here as a process that moves in time, beginning with the selection and admission of students, over a two-year period through a series of processes; classes held, field work, individual conferences, meetings of students, of faculty, of field supervisors, significant, each one, not only in and for itself, but in relation to the way it fits into the whole, and into the process, building on what has gone before carrying what is significant in the living present, anticipating what is to come.

The ending of the educational program has its own importance. Term papers, examinations, theses and research projects, last class sessions, ending conferences with supervisors and with advisers give the student an opportunity to pull together and claim what he has learned and made his own, and so to possess it more fully to use and to commit himself to a continuing professional development as he leaves the school and enters on professional practice.

Social Work's Contribution to Primary and Secondary Education

What does social work have to offer schools that achieves a social work purpose while helping schools realize their own primary purpose as schools, all within the general purpose of helping people to live in and participate in creating a better world? Social workers are trained to work within an institutional framework, and to make some agency's or institution's purposes usable by the clientele served for their own and the community's welfare.

A significant number of children are unable to profit from what the school has to offer, no matter how skillfully it is made available by capable teachers, well-devised programs, and excellent administration. When children fail to learn in accordance with their capacities or when they show by their behavior, whether excessively withdrawn or excessively aggressive, that they are failing to use the social experience of being in school, the school fails of its purpose. Parents, who have their own hopes and purposes in sending children to school, quite apart from school's being a requirement, fail too, in their purposes as *parents* of children in school.

And perhaps most important of all, children fail in their own purpose of growth, which moves however blindly within the most recalcitrant or withdrawn child. They fail in the purpose of self-realization of using the outside world and their own resources. The social worker is possessed of a helping skill which, if she is a part of a school system as school social worker, she can put at the disposal of school, school children, and parents of school children.

Through the method or process of social casework, she is able to work with individual school children who fail to use the school experience fully for learning and growth. The essence of her skill is to help the child feel and express his own distress at the way things are going, and to use her help through sustained conferences within which a relationship develops, to find a better way and a way more rewarding both for him and for the school. In this instance the social worker's learned skill in releasing "idealist will power" is used in an individual-to-individual relationship with a school child so that he may become a self-starter and a self-governor and go forward without her individualized help. Often there may be health problems, or depriving and distressing situations in the home or neighborhood that press heavily on the child and prevent him from receiving the nourishment and support he needs to progress. It is then the social worker's task to help him and his parents get to and use whatever resources exist in the community (and part of the social worker's training is to know what and where they are)—medical, psychiatric, financial assistance, child care or whatever.

With the parents of school children, too, the social worker can use her skill, to help them discover and act on their own wish to be good parents of children in school, and through their relationship with their children to further their growth, and specifically their growth in school and use of school for learning. How frequently and over how long a time parents are seen by the social worker will depend on the requirements of the individual situation. But once again, it is the relationship skill that is used, as parents develop trust in the worker sufficient to try to find a new way of relating to a child in school that will be more rewarding for them as parents and more usable by the child in his school life.

With the school and its personnel the social worker has a different kind of relationship. As an employee of the school, she is in it and of it. Her purpose, therefore, is identical with the school's: to make it "work" for children; and specifically for those children for whom it is presently *not* working to their or its satisfaction. But she has her distinctive social work knowledge and skill to bring to the school's accomplishment of its purpose as school. It is different from the skill of the classroom teacher, the principal, the school nurse or any of the others who form the school team. As a colleague, she shares with the teacher her understanding of what has gone awry in a child that has resulted in the school problem. She shares what she plans to do, and as time goes on she also shares what she is doing with the child and his family, and within the community and its agencies and resources. The teacher is free to use this understanding of an individual child to find her own way in modifying her approach to him as classroom teacher if that seems indicated. She will know better than the school social worker what she as classroom teacher can do that could be helpful to this particular kind of child with this particular kind of problem.

If a change in program or placement within the school seems indicated the principal is in a position to know both what is desirable and possible, in the light of what the school social worker, the classroom teacher, and others of the school faculty, such as the psychologist, can tell him of this particular child and his needs.

The contribution of the school social worker to the school is not limited solely to casework help involving individual-to-individual counseling with the child and his parents. Social workers trained in social group work or with some understanding of social group work have proved helpful in working with groups of children toward their more satisfactory school adjustment. In the public schools of Baltimore, a school social worker has been meeting with groups of children who have come before the court for truancy. These children, in weekly group meetings with the school social worker, are sharing their frustrations and discontents and trying, with the social work leader's help to discover some wish and capacity in themselves to stay in school and do something productive with it. School social workers with skills in social group work can also be effective in working with groups of parents or teachers and such programs are already in operation. What the social worker knows of principles of community organization also helps her represent the school, as one highly significant social institution in the community, and bring it into working relationship with other institutions and groups interested in working toward a better community for all people.

If the social worker is not the school's own, but is an employee of some other community agency, whether family counseling, court, clinic or other, she still has a relationship skill to bring to working with school children and their parents as she helps them find a more satisfying and socially productive place for themselves in the community, but her purpose is dictated by the specific purpose of the agency employing her. It lacks the sharp focus on the child's school experience. The social worker's identification with the school's own purpose is less strong, and she is less available to the school for its use both in service to its children and for rethinking its program as it serves all children.

Schools are best served by social work when they employ their own social workers. Such workers serve the school's own children in relation to school-centered problems, and co-operate with and enlist the help of social workers making other community services available, in the interest of the school's children and their families.

CONDITIONS FURTHERING THE CONTRIBUTION OF SOCIAL WORK
TO EDUCATION

Social work and education can best work together when they understand and respect each other, when each recognizes the other's differences, and when both are committed to broad common goals. There should also be an appreciation that since the specific purposes of primary and secondary education and social work are necessarily different, the competencies developed through their educational programs must also be different.

Values reflected in respect for human dignity, appreciation of individual differences, the importance accorded the development of individual capacity within a social situation (school or world) that furthers such development, should not be hard to agree on. If each profession trusts the other to do its own job and in so doing to contribute to the doing of the common job, the groundwork for fruitful collaboration has been laid. A further requirement is that each appreciate the significance of the other's job; this is just as important for social work, which must value the school and its contribution to a good society, as it is for the school which must value social work, and its contribution to a good society.

Within the school situation, the school can show its appreciation of the value of social work by providing the kind of facilities the social worker needs to do her job well: a private office for interviewing, secretarial help for appropriate record-keeping, and administrative arrangements that assure an orderly referral and reporting process. With mutual respect and understanding the way can be found for the school to realize the best that social work can bring to it.

As the two professions work together perhaps they can hope to answer affirmatively the question posed by Joseph Wood Krutch in *Human Nature and the Human Condition:* "The Twentieth Century—Dawn or Twilight?" [5] The social worker and the teacher, each in his own way and together, can help it to be dawn for those whose lives they touch and for the world in which they live.

---

[5] Joseph Wood Krutch, *Human Nature and the Human Condition* (New York: Random House, 1959).

4

EDUCATION OF TEACHERS: SOCIAL FOUNDATIONS

By I. James Quillen

The social foundations of education have their roots in the inter-relationships between sociology and education. Sociology, for some time, has contributed to the professional preparation of both educators and social workers. In fact, there is much common ground in the content of sociology that has pertinence for both social work and education and, therefore, can help provide a channel for more effective communication between the two fields in their common task of more effectively meeting the needs of children and youth. This opportunity has been recognized in both Europe and the United States. In 1961, the Fourth Interprofessional Conference of Teachers and Social Workers in Great Britain had as its theme "The Teaching of Sociology to Students of Education and Social Work." [1]

A brief consideration of the interrelationships between education and society and culture will help to illuminate the development and nature of the social foundations as a field of study. It is difficult to understand the nature of the social foundations of education without a knowledge of its origin and development. The field, even today, lacks sharpness of focus and agreement on definition, objectives, and content. It is not even designated by a common name. Educational sociology, the social foundations of education, and the sociology of education are all used as names for the field. Some educators use these names interchangeably, but historically, each name has a separate origin and a somewhat distinctive meaning. Educational sociology was the first name widely used to designate the field, and

---

[1] Paul Halmos, ed., "The Teaching of Sociology to Students of Education and Social Work," *Sociological Review*, Monograph No. 4 (Keele: University College of North Staffordshire, July 1961).

it was coined in the 1890's as a result of the growing concern of sociologists and educators about the social role of the school.

The Social Role of the School

A useful definition of education is that it changes individual behavior in some desirable direction. Whether behavior is desirable or not is determined by the values that guide the educational process—by some conception of the good individual and the good society. Education is the process through which the potentialities of the individual are developed and by which societies and cultures perpetuate themselves and more fully realize their values. It is the process by which individuals acquire the skills, knowledge, and values needed to maintain and improve themselves and the society of which they are a part. It involves cultural transmission and socialization. It is furthered best through identification with good models, richness in experience, and effective communication. When any of these is absent or limited severely in the home, neighborhood, or school, the process of education is hampered.

All societies and cultures contain a variety of educative agencies. In American culture, these include the family, peer groups, mass media, the church, child- and youth-serving agencies, and the community as a whole, as well as the school. The unique characteristic of the school is that it is established and maintained for the sole purpose of education.

Schools are established in societies and cultures whenever other educative agencies are not developing adequately the skills, knowledge, and values necessary to maintain their ways of living. The more complex the society and culture, the more significant is the role of the school. The increasing complexity and rapidity of change in contemporary scientific-technological, industrial-urban culture has greatly enhanced the importance of the school both to the individual and society. If the school is to serve this role effectively, however, teachers must be aware of other educative agencies in the culture and their effects on the behavior of the young. Teachers and other school personnel need to join their efforts with workers in other agencies who are seeking to meet educational needs. It is in this context that improved communication between teachers and social workers becomes increasingly important.

Education of the Teacher

Industrial-urban culture has made both the school system and the task of the teacher more complex and has increased the importance of teacher education. The individual preparing to become a teacher needs a broad liberal education; breadth and depth of knowledge in a teaching field; an understanding of the interrelationship of the school and contemporary society and culture, and of the school as a social system; knowledge of individual growth and development, individual differences, learning, and measurement; competence in curricular organization, teaching methods, and the use of appropriate materials; and directed clinical experiences in the classroom and school. The major educational elements in teacher preparation are (1) general education; (2) specialization in a teaching field or fields; (3) the foundations of education; (4) curriculum and instruction; and (5) clinical experiences, such as student teaching or an internship.

Educational psychology and the social foundations of education have become the two major foundation fields in many programs of teacher education,with the former concentrating on the individual learner and the latter on societal and cultural factors involved in the educational program. The philosophy of education, history of education, and comparative education are other important foundational fields included in many teacher education programs.

Educational Sociology As a Field of Study

Educational sociology was the name first given to the field now known as the social foundations of education. Educational sociology developed out of the ideas of such men as Lester Ward and John Dewey in the United States and Emile Durkheim in Europe. As early as 1883, Lester Ward gave major attention to education in the last chapter of his well-known book, *Dynamic Sociology*.

The 1890's have been called the watershed of American history. It was a period of rapid transition to an industrial and urban culture in the United States. Critical social problems became only too apparent both in rural areas and the industrial city—the new power center in American culture. In the colleges and universities there was rapid development in the social sciences, especially sociology, and in the professional study of education. Both sociologists and educators became vitally concerned about the social role of the school. In 1893, William T. Harris, the United States Commissioner of Education, asserted that "no philosophy of education is sound . . . unless based upon sociology." [2] By 1895, courses in sociology for teachers were being offered at New York University and Stanford.

In 1897, John Dewey submitted to William Rainey Harper a plan for organizing work in a department of pedagogy at the University of Chicago. He proposed that professional education be divided into

---

[2] J. S. Roucek, "Some Contributions of Sociology to Education," in H. E. Barnes *et al.*, eds., *Contemporary Social Theory* (New York: Appleton-Century, 1940), p. 798.

five main areas, one of which he labeled "educational sociology." This is the first known use of the term. Dewey proposed that the area concern itself "with the organization and administration of the educational system, both in relation to other social conditions and institutions and in its own external mechanism and workings." [3] The first authenticated course named educational sociology was offered by Henry Suzzallo at Teachers College, Columbia University, in 1910.[4]

By the 1920's a number of colleges and universities were offering educational sociology as a major course in the preparation of teachers. The area continued to expand in the 1930's and was often associated with educational psychology as a foundational course in teacher education. As educational sociology developed as an area of study, it was taught generally by professional educators rather than sociologists. The courses offered often lacked focus and tended to be diffuse and hortatory. Few sociologists maintained a serious interest in the field, and in 1948 the section on educational sociology of the American Sociological Society was temporarily discontinued.

NATURE OF EDUCATIONAL SOCIOLOGY

The first major emphasis in educational sociology was philosophical. The focus was on the use of sociology to identify the social role and objectives of the school; the school was conceived as an instrument of social control and social progress. In this sense it may be said that educational sociology emerged out of a milieu of social reform and had origins closely allied with those of the field of social work.

Applied sociology was added early in the organization of courses in educational sociology. Concepts, principles, and methods from the social sciences were applied to formal education, including the curriculum, methods of teaching, discipline, and school administration.

At New York University in the 1920's a functional approach to educational sociology developed. This approach stressed social behavior and sought to make educational sociology a more integral part of sociology itself. The functional approach focused on the interac-

---

[3] John Dewey, "Plan for organization of work in a fully equipped Department of Pedagogy, memorandum to W. R. Harper, January 6, 1897 (microfilm, University of Chicago archives, Roll 3, WRH 86). Copy courtesy of W. H. Cowley.

[4] Irene J. Lawrence, "A History of Educational Sociology in the United States," pp. 31–32. Unpublished Ph.D. dissertation, Stanford University, 1951. Another useful study of the history of educational sociology, in addition to Roucek and Lawrence, is Brigham Young Card, "American Educational Sociology from 1890 to 1950—A Sociological Analysis." Unpublished Ph.D. dissertation, Stanford University, 1959. All of these have been drawn upon in summarizing the historical background and describing the nature of educational sociology in this paper.

tion of individuals in various kinds of groups and the effects of this interaction on social behavior. The causes of social maladjustment and antisocial behavior in children were studied. Casework and group techniques were used to improve the social adjustment of children. The role of social agencies in the community in meeting the needs of children was stressed. The control of the environment was considered of primary importance in the educational process. Social interaction in slums, gangs, immigrant groups, and families was studied.

In 1932, Willard Waller in his book, *The Sociology of Teaching*, attempted to make educational sociology a descriptive science. Robert Cooley Angell, Florian Znaniecki, and E. B. Reuter held similar views. As early as 1928, Angell wrote that "educational sociology is . . . merely a branch of the pure science of sociology." [5] In order to separate the field from the idea of social reform, he recommended that it be called the sociology of education. Those who wanted to make educational sociology a descriptive science emphasized social interaction within the school and between the school and the larger society.

This brief summary of the development of educational sociology illustrates the different points of view and approaches that were included in the field and elements that should be included in a definition of it. John A. Kinneman, even though he had described educational sociology as "the scientific approach to a social philosophy of education," defined it more broadly by writing in 1932: "It is . . . that body of social knowledge, together with the techniques for enlarging and applying the knowledge, which can be used to advantage in the educational process." [6] From the point of view of teacher education, the field can be said to include the knowledge, methods of thinking, and techniques of research from the social sciences which can assist the teacher in better understanding his task and in performing it more effectively. Educational sociology has emphasized such things as the interrelationships between education and society and culture, the role of the school in the realization of democratic values, the society and culture of the school, the forces outside the school affecting the education of children and youth, and the application of knowledge and methods from the social sciences to educational problems.

PURPOSES OF EDUCATIONAL SOCIOLOGY

In 1947, George S. Herrington made a careful national survey

---

[5] Robert Cooley Angell, "Science, Sociology, and Education," *Journal of Educational Sociology*, Vol. 1, No. 7 (March 1928), pp. 406–413.

[6] John A. Kinneman, *Society and Education* (New York: Macmillan Company, 1932), pp. 48–49.

called "Educational Sociology as a Factor in the Training of Teachers." [7] He found that some 150 objectives were listed for required or partly required courses in educational sociology. The five most often cited objectives listed in order of frequency were:

1. Understanding the role of the school as an instrument of social progress
2. The meaning of democracy
3. Understanding social problems
4. Understanding school-community relations
5. The use of techniques of research and critical thinking [8]

Most of the objectives cited stressed knowledge and understanding. There was no direct reference to the development of attitudes, and only three of the objectives listed stressed skills and abilities.

In analyzing the content of the courses in educational sociology, Herrington found that the twelve topics most often included in them, listed by order of frequency, were:

1. The community and the school
2. Pressure groups, public opinion, propaganda, and education
3. Education and the family
4. Intercultural education
5. Democracy and education
6. Leisure, recreation, and education
7. The meaning and functions of educational sociology
8. The church and education
9. Health and education
10. Crime, delinquency, and education
11. The social function of the school
12. Occupational trends and their educational implications [9]

In comparing the topics he found most frequently included in educational sociology courses with those found by Harvey Lee in a study made in 1926, Herrington concluded that more emphasis was being given after World War II to school-community relationships and the role of the teacher in the community. Among other topics given greater emphasis were: intercultural education; crime, delinquency, and education; and health and education. This study shows the increasing congruence of emphases in the field of educational sociology and social work by the end of World War II.

In the early 1940's there was a decline in offerings in educational sociology and in emphasis on it in the preparation of teachers. This

---

[7] George S. Herrington, "Educational Sociology as a Factor in the Training of Teachers." Unpublished Ed.D. dissertation, Stanford University, 1947.

[8] *Ibid.*, p. 147.

[9] *Ibid.*

was, in part, due to the lack of focus and the weakness in research and scholarship in the field. Too many professors of educational sociology were inadequately trained in sociology itself. Too few sociologists were interested in research in education. Even though Herrington found greater agreement on the nature and functions of educational sociology than did Lee, the objectives and topics stressed in teacher education courses still showed great diffuseness and a general lack of a clearly defined structure. In 1937, David Snedden had referred to the field as "immature and unstandardized." [10] In the second edition of the *Encyclopedia of Educational Research,* published in 1950, Lloyd Allen Cook could still refer to:

> ... the inevitable marginality of the field, its continued lack of research emphasis, its still limited contributions to teacher education, and the tendency of theorists to add bits of sociology to bits of education rather than to attempt to build a new, functional discipline.[11]

In spite of such criticisms, the area of professional education concerned with the study of the social aspects of schooling has shown surprising vitality. This has been due to what might seem on the surface to be two conflicting trends in the field, which have actually tended to reinforce each other. The first of these trends is the broadening of the conception of the field under the label of the social foundations of education, and the second has been the emergence of a sharper focus and a more concerted emphasis on the field within the discipline of sociology under the name of the sociology of education. Both of these developments involve a greater interest in the study of education by social scientists in a number of disciplines.

Social Foundations of Education

The term "social foundations of education" gained prominence at Teachers College, Columbia University, during the 1930's. The title of one of the reports of the Commission on the Social Studies of the American Historical Association, written by George S. Counts and others, was *The Social Foundations of Education.*[12] The report was concerned with the social backgrounds of American education. In 1933, courses formerly included in educational sociology at Columbia were included in the offerings of the new Department of

---

[10] *Ibid.,* p. 2. Quoted from David Snedden, "The Field of Educational Sociology," *Review of Educational Research,* Vol. 7, No. 1 (February 1937), p. 10.

[11] Lloyd A. Cook, "Educational Sociology," in Walter S. Monroe, ed., *Encyclopedia of Educational Research* (rev. ed.; New York: Macmillan Company, 1950), p. 352.

[12] George S. Counts *et al., The Social Foundations of Education* (New York: Charles Scribner's Sons, 1934).

Sociological and Economic Foundations; in 1943 the name of the department was changed to Social Foundations; and in 1946 the triennial issue of the *Review of Educational Research* devoted to the interrelationships between education and society was titled "The Social Foundations of Education." [13] Since then, this name has been adopted in a number of colleges and universities to replace educational sociology. "Social foundations" has a broader connotation than "educational sociology." It is concerned with the contributions of all the social sciences to an understanding of the interaction of educational institutions and the larger society. As Lawrence points out:

> It was thought that sociology alone could not give a complete picture of the interaction of culture and education but that the other social sciences including economics, government, anthropology, and social psychology also needed to be studied and coordinated with education.[14]

The term social foundations of education has become more popular since World War II, in part because social scientists in many fields have become more interested in studying educational problems. Anthropologists, for example, have become more interested in the role of education in culture, cultural transmission, cross-cultural studies of education, acculturation, and the like. George D. Spindler has recently brought together the work of a number of anthropologists under the title *Education and Culture: Anthropological Approaches*.[15] He points out that anthropology has only recently begun to make a significant contribution to the social foundations of education. As he states, the encyclopedic *Anthropology Today*, edited by Alfred Kroeber in 1953, did not even include education as an area of anthropological application.[16] However, several universities now have anthropologists who are participating in teacher education programs and doing research and teaching such courses in the social foundations area as "Cultural Transmission" and "Social Anthropology in Education." As Spindler says of anthropology and education:

> The core of the contribution is in the attention to culture as a behavioral compulsive, as a perception-directing set of patterns, and in the attention to the variable forms these patterns take.

---

13 Lawrence, *op. cit.*, pp. 113–134.

14 *Ibid.*, pp. 133–134.

15 George D. Spindler, "Anthropology and Education: An Overview," in Spindler, *Education and Anthropology* (Stanford, Calif.: Stanford University Press, 1955), p. 11.

16 Alfred Kroeber, ed., *Anthropology Today* (Chicago: University of Chicago Press, 1953).

Cultural awareness is one vital aim of each course, but not merely generalized cultural awareness; the aim is to create in the teacher an awareness of how culture influences specifically what he does as a teacher and how to think about, observe, and analyze this influence.[17]

Economists, too, are becoming increasingly interested in the economic aspects of education, and a number of significant publications are appearing on this subject. Some of the educational topics in which economists have shown interest are the role of education in economic growth, the labor force and education, investment in education, and education and the process of social selection and mobility. A. H. Halsey, Jean Floud, and C. Arnold Anderson have recently brought together the writings on education of a number of economists and others under the title *Education, Economy, and Society: A Reader in the Sociology of Education.* They point out:

> In an advanced industrial society, it is inevitable that the educational system should come into very close relationship with the economy. Modern industrial technology . . . is dependent to an unprecedented extent on the results of scientific research, on the supply of skilled and responsible manpower, and consequently on the efficiency of the educational system.[18]

In writing of the "Sociology of Talent," Halsey, Floud, and Anderson state:

> Unequal life-chances are both cause and effect of unequal educational opportunities; but social factors intrude on the edutional process in more subtle ways than implied in this statement. . . . Widespread social amelioration since World War II has not removed persistent class and ethnic inequalities in the distribution of ability (potential) and attainment (performance). The emphasis in investigation has shifted in recent years, from study of the material disabilities traditionally underlying these inequalities, to attempts, on the one hand, to identify social factors impinging on the intellectual development of individuals and, on the other hand, to explore the social and cultural circumstances affecting their attainment or performance at a given level of ability.[19]

Hence, new insights are emerging into the problem of identifying and developing the talent required for the effective operation of an industrial-urban society based on scientific advancement.

---

[17] Spindler, *op. cit.*, pp. 65–66.

[18] A. H. Halsey, J. Floud, and C. A. Anderson, *Education, Economy, and Society: A Reader in the Sociology of Education* (New York: Free Press of Glencoe, 1961), p. 1.

[19] *Ibid.*, p. 7.

Political scientists also are beginning to give more attention to the field of education. Some of the areas in education that are of concern to political scientists are the relation of education to different political systems, the political control of education, and education and the law. The recent drive against racial discrimination in education, the increased concern over civil rights and liberties, and the growing controversy over the separation of the church and state in education have focused increased attention on the legal aspects of education.

The recent book by Gabriel A. Almond and Sidney Verba, *The Civic Culture: Political Attitudes and Democracy in Five Nations,* is an example of how political science can contribute to the social foundations of education. This is a study of the political culture of democracy and the relevance of such a study to the role of education in a democracy is clear. In their preface, the authors state:

> We are concerned in this book with a number of classic themes of political science: with what the Greeks called civic virtue and its consequences for the effectiveness and stability of the democratic polity; and with the kind of community life, social organization, and upbringing of children that fosters civic virtue.[20]

Research, writing, and teaching in social psychology have made significant contributions to the social foundations of education as well as to educational sociology and the sociology of teaching. The Society for the Psychological Study of Social Issues recently produced a book of *Readings in the Social Psychology of Education.*[21] The readings in it were organized under the following topics: social class and family influences; school desegregation; school and campus learning environments; student relationships in the classroom; teacher-student interaction; student motivation and teacher control; shaping attitudes through schools; the American teacher; and adults in the school and community. Most of these topics might legitimately be included in a course on the social foundations of education, and some of them are also included in courses in educational psychology.

Thus, the content of the social foundations of education draws from anthropology, economics, political science, and social psychology. It also includes content and methods from sociology, cultural and social history, and social philosophy. The sociology of educa-

---

[20] Gabriel A. Almond and Sidney Verba, *The Civic Culture: Political Attitudes and Democracy in Five Nations* (Princeton, N.J.: Princeton University Press, 1963), p. vii.

[21] W. W. Charters, Jr., and N. L. Gage, eds., *Readings in the Social Psychology of Education* (Boston: Allyn and Bacon, 1963).

tion also draws content from some of these fields, especially sociology and social psychology.

Sociology of Education

Since World War II, Wilbur B. Brookover has taken leadership in building a sociology of education on the basis of the ideas advanced by Willard Waller, Robert C. Angell, Florian Znaniecki, and E. B. Reuter. In 1955 he published a basic textbook entitled *A Sociology of Education*. In it he asserted:

> [The] sociology of education *is* the scientific analysis of the social processes and social patterns involved in the educational system. This assumes that education is a combination of social acts and that sociology is the analysis of human interaction. Such analysis of human interaction in education may include both the formal education occurring in social groups such as the school and the multitude of informal communication processes which serve educational functions. It is also assumed that such an analysis leads to development of scientific generalizations about human relations in the educational system. Finally, any adequate sociology of education must present hypotheses concerning such human relations which will provide the body of theory to be tested in research.[22]

The new emphasis on the sociology of education is furthered by the increase in basic research on educational problems by sociologists. The American Sociological Society reformed its section on educational sociology in 1950, and in 1958 the Russell Sage Foundation published a summary of such research under the title *Sociology and the Field of Education,* prepared by Orville G. Brim, Jr. Brim was able to identify over a hundred basic sociological research references on education. He organized these research studies under the headings: the aims of education; the allocation of materials; the allocation of personnel (educators and students); roles in the institution (educators and students); the functions of education; and the roles of the sociologists in educational training and research. He concluded:

> [Since 1950] there had been a rapid growth of interest in studies of the educational institution; and in recent years a greater number of both well-established and younger sociologists competent to carry on research programs of good quality have moved into this area. Standards of research have risen, and recognized areas of sociological theory pertaining to social class, small groups, roles, and occupational mobility, to name

---

[22] Wilbur B. Brookover, *A Sociology of Education* (New York: American Book Co., 1955), p. 31.

but a few, are being brought to bear on the several aspects of the educational system.[23]

Jean Floud and A. H. Halsey also summarized in 1958 the research in the sociology of education for *Current Sociology,* a publication of the International Sociological Association.[24] They were able to identify a significant number of research studies in the field which had been published both in Europe and the United States. Another significant indication of the growing interest of sociologists in the field is that in the summer of 1963, the American Sociological Association took over publication of the *Journal of Educational Sociology,* founded by E. George Payne in 1927, and changed its name to *Sociology of Education.* In a statement of editorial policy, the association said it "intends to provide a forum for studies of education by scholars in all the social sciences from all parts of the world." The statement, while highly encouraging, shows how difficult it will be to maintain a distinction between the sociology of education and the social foundations of education.

The sociology of education is concerned with education from several points of view. One of these is a consideration of the school in the larger social structure. This involves a study of values, demography, social and political systems—all within a context of change and development. This has been called the macrocosmic level of the sociology of education. Another level is the study of schools and classrooms as social systems and subcultures. This has been called the microcosmic level. Sociologists of education also are interested in forces and groups outside the school—such as the family, neighborhood, church, and social class—which affect the educative process. The center of attention in both in-school and out-of-school contexts is the socialization of the child—the internalization of the moral commitments and the capacity to be an effective member of the larger society and culture. Finally, the sociology of education is concerned with teaching as an occupation and a career.[25]

These areas of content and analysis can be summarized as follows:

1. Educational institutions in the larger social structure
2. The school and classroom as social systems
3. External forces and groups affecting the educative process

---

[23] Orville G. Brim, Jr., *Sociology and the Field of Education* (New York: Russell Sage Foundation, 1958), pp. 110–111.

[24] Jean Floud and A. H. Halsey, "The Sociology of Education," *Current Sociology,* Vol. 7, No. 3 (1958), entire issue.

[25] Floud and Halsey, *op. cit.,* p. 170; *see also* Neal Gross, "The Sociology of Education," in Robert K. Merton *et al.,* eds., *Sociology Today: Problems and Prospects* (New York: Basic Books, 1959), pp. 131–152; and Neal Gross, "Some Contributions of Sociology to the Field of Education," *Harvard Educational Review,* Vol. 29, No. 4 (Fall 1959), pp. 275–287.

4. The socialization of the child
5. Teaching as an occupation and profession

As examples of the approaches used by sociologists of education, points 2 and 3 will be discussed briefly. Floud and Halsey have stated in relation to these two areas that the task of sociologists

> ... is to analyze the social factors which influence the educational process from two main sources ... those ... deriving from the family environment and general background of teachers and pupils ... and ... those deriving from the social organization, formal and informal, of schools, colleges, and universities. In practice, the educability of an individual, given his personal endowment and unique life-history, is a function of the interaction of all these *social* factors; that is to say, it represents his socially determined capacity to respond to the demands of the particular educational arrangements to which he is exposed.[26]

C. Wayne Gordon has investigated the social system of a midwestern high school. He divided the high school social system into three subsystems: (1) the formal bureaucratic organization focused on academic achievement; (2) the semiformal system focused on sponsored student organizations concerned with extracurricular activities; and (3) the informal system of interpersonal friendship relationships among pupils characterized by the "clique" or "crowd." Gordon found that the pupil was motivated basically by his desire to achieve and maintain status in the school society and that his behavior in any particular situation is the result of his standing in the school status system. He concluded that "it is the adolescent's ability to perceive and fulfill the expectations of the school, which determine his adjustment to the school rather than his [social] class position." He found that the *"dominant orientation to action was to accept those roles which would establish a prestige position in the informal organization."* [27]

Gordon found dropouts resulted either from the failure to achieve and maintain status in the school culture or from influences outside the schools. Boys tended to drop out because they could not meet minimum grade standards, while girls were more likely to be influenced by failure to meet other expectations. He concluded that:

> The system of adolescent organization in this school situation is best characterized as a system of action based on efforts to achieve a differentiated social status, because life as a member

---

[26] Floud and Halsey, *op. cit.,* p. 183.
[27] C. Wayne Gordon, *The Social System of the High School: A Study in the Sociology of Adolescence* (Glencoe, Ill.: The Free Press, 1957), pp. 1–2, 22.

of the undifferentiated mass is unbearable. The pupil eventually had to exist in this situation with the protection of group membership which made him a visible, active *"somebody,"* whose image was reflected upon himself through the eyes of those who viewed him, presumably with enough esteem to give him the necessary potency to act in a highly competitive environment. Oblivion may be worse than infamy.[28]

The "climate of values" of the "society of adolescents" in nine midwestern public high schools in small towns, cities, and suburbs was studied by James S. Coleman. His findings tended to confirm those of Gordon. He found that as there is more to learn in a complex industrial society and formal education becomes more important to success, adolescent culture "shows little interest in education" and focuses the attention of teenagers on other things such as "cars, dates, sports, and popular music." [29] Scholastic success was not highly valued. The norms of the teenage culture thus often tend to work against the academic values of the teacher. To meet this situation, Coleman recommended more emphasis on interscholastic and intramural group competition in the achievement of scholastic goals and less emphasis on individual competition for grades.[30]

The social system of the school class has been analyzed by Talcott Parsons. He asserted that the school class had the dual function of socialization and selection: (1) the internalization in pupils of the "commitments and capacities for the successful performance of their future adult roles"; and (2) to allocate them "within the role-structure of the adult society." These functions are interrelated. The task is to develop a commitment to the *"values of society"* and "to the performance of a specific type of role within the *structure* of society." He analyzes the relationship of the family and peer group to the work of the school and the differentiation of function of the elementary and secondary schools. He concludes:

> [The] elementary school phase is concerned with the internalization in children of motivation to achievement, and the selection of persons on the basis of differential capacity for achievement. The focus is on the *level* of capacity. In the secondary school phase, on the other hand, the focus is on the differentiation of qualitative types of achievement.[31]

---

[28] *Ibid.,* pp. 24–25.

[29] James S. Coleman, "Academic Achievement and the Structure of Competition," *Harvard Educational Review,* Vol. 29, No. 4 (Fall 1959), p. 330. Reprinted in Halsey, Floud, and Anderson, *op. cit.*

[30] *Ibid.,* pp. 348–351.

[31] Talcott Parsons, "The School Class As a Social System," *Harvard Educational Review,* Vol. 29, No. 4 (Fall 1959), p. 313. Reprinted in Halsey, Floud, and Anderson, *op. cit.*

Course Content

Lacking a recent survey of the content in courses in the social foundations of education, the best sources of information are currently used textbooks.[32] The topics listed below are illustrative of those that would be found typically in social foundations courses for teachers:

A. Education in American society and culture

1. The nature of American culture and its values, the rapidity of social change, and the role of the school in an industrial-urban culture based on science and technology
2. The structure of American society, social stratification, and social mobility
3. The role of the school in selecting individuals for various positions and roles in society

B. The socialization of the child

1. The family and the educational process; the role of the family in cultural transmission, enculturation, socialization, and personality development; the wide range of family patterns in the United States and their effects on the education of the young
2. The peer group as an educative agency; its function of cross-fertilization in cultural transmission and in shaping of values
3. The society and culture of the school; the school as an institution deliberately fashioned for the sole purpose of education; the social systems of the school and classroom
4. Out-of-school educative agencies other than family and peer groups: the mass media, child- and youth-serving agencies; and the social climate of the neighborhood and community

C. The school and the community

1. Trends in population composition and mobility; the educational effects of rapidity of population growth and high mobility; larger families and more transient children
2. The changing pattern of urbanization; the exodus of the middle class from the large cities, the growth of suburbia and the urban region, and the movement of lower socio-

---

[32] Particular use has been made of Robert J. Havighurst and Bernice L. Neugarten, *Society and Education* (2d ed.; Boston: Allyn and Bacon, 1962), and Brookover, *op. cit.* A revised edition of the latter was published in 1964. *See* Wilbur B. Brookover and David Gottlieb, *A Sociology of Education* (2d ed.; New York: American Book Company, 1964).

economic groups from rural areas to the centers of large cities, with the consequent spread of slums; school dropouts and juvenile delinquency; urban redevelopment and the efforts to increase equality of opportunity

3. Minority group segregation and discrimination; the role of the school in social integration, the equalization of opportunity, and the improvement of intergroup relations; the education of the socially disadvantaged

4. Education as an instrument of international relations; the growing international importance of education; education and economic growth; the international movement of students and educators; the school as a bastion of national defense and as an agency for developing international understanding

5. The changing occupational patterns; automation; high occupational mortality; the increasing demand for workers at the highest levels of talent and education; the role of the school in vocational education

D. The teacher

1. The teacher in school and community
2. Teaching as a career
3. Education as a profession

This outline of content in the social foundations of education includes a number of areas of interest and concern to both teachers and social workers. Both education and social work are concerned with the values of American culture, and an understanding of the values and the ways in which they are changing provides a sound basis for communication and co-operation between the two professions. The rapidity of social change, with its accompanying social lag and maladjustments, affects the roles of both educators and social workers. An understanding of the class structure of American society, with the differing cultures of the lower and middle classes, helps to illuminate the social and educational problems of many children and youth. Equality of educational opportunity often involves both an amelioration of the home environment as well as action within the school.

Both social workers and teachers are vitally concerned with the variety of American family patterns. For both professions, the family is a central institution which affects their work. Peer group associations, next to the family, are perhaps the most important force in the socialization of the young. Personality stability and instability, good character and delinquency, and motivation for or against learning often have their roots in peer group participation.

Peer group relations carry over from the neighborhood to the school, and vice versa. Both Gordon and Coleman found that striving for peer group status in the social system of the school is a most important force in motivating and controlling pupil behavior. Dropouts often are directly related to lack of success in the social system of the school. The importance of out-of-school agencies in the education of the young makes it imperative for teachers and social workers to have common understandings and effective communication if maximum educational achievement and welfare are to be realized. The community climate of opinion affects everyone who is concerned with individual and group improvement. Children and youth tend to accept as norms the standards of behavior that bring rewards and prestige in the larger community.

The changing pattern of American urban life is shaping the environment within which both teachers and social workers seek to achieve their goals. The larger size of many families and the increasing number of transient children in American urban communities affect both education and social welfare. The movement of the middle class to the suburbs and the influx of lower socioeconomic groups from rural areas is changing the character of American cities. The culturally disadvantaged, the socially alienated, the dropout, and urban poverty are major concerns for schools as well as for social workers. The rising expectations of minority groups are dramatizing these problems for all Americans and creating powerful forces for social change in urban life and education. Equalization of opportunity is gaining new meaning and social integration new strength, as pressures increase from many directions. The concern for equalization of opportunity and the raising of welfare levels has become an important factor in education at the international level. Finally, the demand for highly talented and educated workers makes the equalization of educational opportunity, increasing motivation for learning among the socially disadvantaged, and school dropouts matters of national concern. Social workers and teachers need to co-operate to make both the community and the school places where children of all backgrounds can make their way and become effective individuals and citizens.

Problems and Limitations of Social Foundations

Even though research and course organization in the social foundations of education have improved since World War II, criticism has continued. James B. Conant, in the report of his recent study of teacher education, was highly critical of the field. He asserted:

> If a competent sociologist is investigating social problems closely related to the schools and is ready to give a course in

educational sociology, the desirability of such a course is evident. As to whether the present group of professors who consider themselves educational sociologists should perpetuate
themselves, I have the gravest doubts.[33]

Although this seems to be too dim a view of the quality of the
educators who are concerned with the relations between education
and society, there is little doubt that limitations exist and further
improvement is needed.

A clearer definition of the nature of the social foundations of
education and its relationship to the sociology of education is
needed. Courses still often lack a sharpness of focus. The progression of learning from the simple to the more complex concepts and
generalizations in the field is still far from clear. Beginning and
advanced courses often lack developmental progression in learning
and sometimes are much too similar and repetitious.

There can be little doubt of the value of content and methods
from the social sciences for teacher education. Teacher competence
involves an increasingly deeper knowledge of the interrelationships
between society and formal education and of the school itself as a
social system. As Floud and Halsey assert, in technological societies
the contribution of education

> to the vast . . . atomized structures . . . is difficult to determine
> . . . it plays a role in relation to all aspects of social structure—
> demographic, economic, political and social, as well as ideo-
> logical or spiritual . . . . In short, industrialism gives rise to—
> or at least, justifies—the sociology of education.[34]

Both educational sociology and the social foundations of education
become more important as society becomes more complex and culture becomes more scientific, technological, and urban.

As the field of the social foundations of education develops, it is
probable that specialization may increase. The anthropology of
education and the economics of education are already beginning
to emerge along with the sociology of education. As this develops
further, the incorporation of courses from these and other social
sciences into the program of teacher education may become an issue
in professional education, and the competition between different
specializations for the limited time available may increase.

Any development that will increase the attention of social scientists to the nature and problems of education in contemporary
society and culture should be encouraged. Education is both an
individual and a social process. To be effective, it must rest on an

---

[33] James B. Conant, *The Education of American Teachers* (New York: Mc-
Graw-Hill Book Co., 1963), p. 131.
[34] Floud and Halsey, *op. cit.*, p. 170.

adequate social as well as a psychological foundation. The ideal situation is for specialists in the social foundations of education to be competent in both the social sciences and professional education. In the early twentieth century social scientists devoted little attention to education, and professional educators were left largely to try to develop the field of educational sociology. Today, sociologists and other social scientists are being brought into professional education programs to meet an obvious lack in research, methods of thinking, and theoretical conceptions. Perhaps in the next generation, competence in the social sciences and a knowledge of professional education can be combined in more individuals. It is likely, however, that the need for co-operation will continue and that progress, in the future as in the past, will result when specialists from various fields concerned with common problems work together in the closest harmony and mutual respect. This generalization holds not only for the social sciences and education but for other fields as well. Educators and social workers also can add to their mutual effectiveness as their communication and co-operation in meeting the needs of the young improve.

5

EDUCATION OF TEACHERS: PSYCHOLOGY OF EDUCATION

By N. L. Gage

The objectives of educational psychology are to provide concepts, principles, and facts on which reasoning about educational problems can be based. Such objectives differ from those that aim at providing direct solutions to problems. Some writers hold that educational psychology enhances the hypothesis-making function of the teacher; others see it as providing part of the basis for sound judgments and interpretations of experience.

Educational psychology is a "foundation" course in the same sense that physics and chemistry are foundation courses for engineers. For the latter, such courses do not tell one how to build bridges or design refineries but they do provide the concepts, principles, and facts upon which engineers must base their solutions to particular problems. Considerations other than physical and chemical ones enter into the engineer's work; similarly, considerations other than psychological ones enter into the work of a teacher. In education, the other considerations take such forms as social values, economic necessities, and political factors. But educational psychology gives the prospective teacher the facts, concepts, and principles about human behavior and psychological characteristics that he needs to keep in mind as he teaches, i.e., as he formulates educational objectives, designs activities and experiences that will foster achievement of those objectives, arranges for learners to carry out these activities and undergo these experiences, and then evaluates the degree to which his students have achieved the objectives.

It may be helpful here to look at four uses of knowledge that have been distinguished by Broudy, Smith, and Burnett: [1]

1. The *associative* use of schooling is made when one responds to a question by calling up from memory something or other suggested by a cue; so-called concomitant learnings can often be classified as associative uses of schooling.

2. The *replicative* use of learning is that which permits one to repeat an operation much as it was performed in school; skills of reading, computing, and reciting belong in this group.

3. The *applicative* use of schooling consists in applying knowledge to particular problems of practice, such as the problems of how to teach reading or fractions. The present courses in educational psychology do not generally give much actual practice in this applicative use of knowledge. Most educational psychologists seem implicitly to hold that this use of educational psychology should be relegated for the most part to subsequent stages of the teacher education program—to student teaching and courses in teaching methods and curriculum. But many critics intimate that educational psychology ought to provide much more practice in applicative uses.

4. The *interpretative* use of schooling, whereby one categorizes, conceptualizes, or classifies experience to make it intelligible, denotes especially well the kinds of purposes and values that educational psychologists see in their course. To bring order out of the confusion that a neophyte experiences when he enters a classroom in the role of teacher—that is, to give him a set of psychological concepts and principles by which he can make sense out of classroom occurrences—is the use of educational psychology apparently considered pre-eminent by those who teach and write the books for the course. It may well be that the course ought to be geared more for action and problem-solving rather than merely for orientation and perspective. But as the course now stands, the latter objectives predominate.

The field of educational psychology has been structured repeatedly over the years by various committees of professional associations and by review publications, but these efforts at restructuring by fiat have had much less influence than the textbook writers, whose formulations are used by hundreds of instructors and thousands of prospective teachers. From an examination of the section headings

---

[1] Harry S. Broudy, B. Othanel Smith, and Joe R. Burnett, *Democracy and Excellence in American Secondary Education* (Chicago: Rand McNally Co., 1964), chap. 3.

of several leading textbooks, one can form an impression of the major categories of the course's content.[2]

Although the textbooks differ in the organization, phrasing, and emphasis of their major headings there is no question but that they have much in common. On the basis of the amount of consideration it receives, the topic of *learning* must be put at the heart of the subject. Since learning is a complex process, it is usually broken down into components. After learning, as a theme of almost equal prominence, comes *growth and development in readiness*, i.e., in abilities, interests, and the like. A section or at least a chapter on *emotional and social adjustment*, or mental health, including character development, is usually present. Finally, there is the ubiquitous chapter or section on *measurement and evaluation*.

Learning

Learning, the pre-eminent topic of present-day educational psychology, is usually divided into a set of components; motivation, perception, response, and reward are a representative set. More than twenty years ago, Miller and Dollard set forth a four-component analysis of learning into drive, cue, response, and reward.[3] In order to learn a person must want something, notice something, do something, and get something. The Miller-Dollard analysis is still useful as a summary of common elements in textbook treatments of learning.

The general conception of learning contained in the Miller-Dollard scheme belongs to what is called reinforcement theory. But educational psychologists now make use, more often than not, of identification theory and cognitive theory as well. Identification theorists consider learning to result, at least in major part, from the learner's identification with a model whom he imitates.[4] In the process of such imitation, the learner acquires the patterns of attitude and behavior of his model. Particularly in explaining the learning of attitudes, values, and styles of behavior that are not neces-

---

[2] *See*, for example, Lee J. Cronbach, *Educational Psychology* (2d ed.; New York: Harcourt, Brace & World, 1963); Herbert J. Klausmeier, *Learning and Human Abilities: Educational Psychology* (New York: Harper & Brothers, 1961); Glenn Myers Blair, R. Stewart Jones, and Ray H. Simpson, *Educational Psychology* (2d ed.; New York: Macmillan Company, 1962); and W. C. Morse and G. M. Wingo, *Psychology and Teaching* (2d ed.; Chicago: Scott, Foresman and Co., 1962).

[3] Neal E. Miller and John Dollard, *Social Learning and Imitation* (New Haven: Yale University Press, 1941).

[4] *See*, for example, Albert Bandura, "Social Learning Through Imitation," in Marshall R. Jones, ed., *Nebraska Symposium on Motivation* (Lincoln: University of Nebraska Press, 1962), pp. 211–268.

sarily subject to reward or nonreward in the ordinary sense, the notion of such learning by identification is often used.

Some psychologists regard learning by identification as a variety of learning by reward, the model serving as a social reinforcer. Others consider such learning to be in a class by itself, since the learned behavior seldom displays the kind of gradual approximation to what is desired that is found in classical instances of learning by conditioning.

In a sense, learning by identification can also be considered to belong to the third major family of theories—learning by the restructuring of perceptions and cognitions. When a person identifies with the attitudes of his model, he perceives the linkage between the model and the attitudes as a very tight one. In incorporating into his own thinking and behavior the ideas and behaviors of his model, he is merely reflecting a changed perception of his social environment.

In the third major family of learning theories, learning is regarded as the cognitive or perceptual restructuring of problematical situations. If the environment of things, persons, and ideas has a structure, analogous to the structure of a building, a mathematical proof, or a novel, then it can be perceived and understood. And learning consists in the perception and cognition of such structure.

Learning conceived as the perception or cognition of structures in the environment has definite implications for teaching. Making the structures of ideas to be learned stand out more clearly, providing over-all structures within which part structures can be placed, tying one structure to another with a transitional or connecting idea—all these are strategies that teachers can use in promoting the learning of meaningful organizations of ideas. Many formulations of learning according to conditioning theory, as in attempts to develop principles of programing for teaching machines and programed textbooks, have concealed within them, to a major degree, a cognitive theory of learning.[5]

Growth and Development

Growth and development as a topic in educational psychology deals with those changes that occur in the physical, emotional, social, and intellectual characteristics of persons as a result of influences other than those explicitly arranged in the school. The great independent variable in studies of growth and development is time, or chrono-

---

[5] *See* N. L. Gage, "Toward a Cognitive Theory of Teaching," *Teachers College Record*, Vol. 65, No. 5 (February 1964), pp. 408–412.

logical age, but cultural factors are also considered major independent variables.

First, the study of growth and development reveals what children are like at a given age, and what they are capable of learning at that age. Such knowledge helps teachers plan their work and guides their expectations. But it cannot take the simple form of parallel lists of age levels and corresponding characteristics and behaviors normal for each age. The definition of normal is not that simple, and many factors influence whether a child will be ahead of or behind what is average for his age group.

A second major concern in this area is the issue of nature and nurture. To what extent are the determiners of differences in ability to benefit from schooling to be found in heredity, rather than environment? Insofar as hereditary factors predominate, there is little that can be done to improve children's ability, and schooling should merely be adjusted to individual differences in IQ. But insofar as environment influences IQ and other factors in learning, something can be done about them. Some authors assume that teachers ought to know the nature of the issue, the ways in which evidence on it is sought, and the implications of present knowledge.

If so, the educational psychology course, but more often the prerequisite first course in general psychology, contains material on the physical basis of heredity in chromosomes and genes, the distinction between fraternal and identical twins, and the ways in which twins and persons in other relationships have been studied to throw light on the nature-nurture issue. Students are told about the sizes of the correlation coefficients that are found between persons of different degrees of blood relationship in such characteristics as height, IQ, temperament, and values. They are given the evidence on the ways in which impoverished environments, on the one hand, and emotional and intellectual enrichment of the child's environment, on the other, can make a difference in how he develops.

Another major concern in studying growth and development may be termed social class. The ideal is that American education should serve all children. In the last twenty years, American educational psychologists have become much more aware that lower-class children differ from middle-class children not only economically but in cultural variables that determine development. Hence, such children also differ in the intellectual nurturing provided by their environments, and in attitudes, values, aspirations, and other characteristics that affect readiness for school learning.

One other topic often comes under the heading of growth and development—sex-linked differences, or the differences between boys and girls in abilities, interests, and skills. Here again, the aim is to eliminate erroneous preconceptions on the part of prospective teachers and to inculcate accurate expectations. Such concerns may help American education to reduce the vast waste of female intellectual resources.

Educational Measurement and Evaluation

Measurement and evaluation is the third major topic of present-day educational psychology. It was given most favored treatment by Dr. Conant in his discussion of the proper educational psychology for prospective secondary school teachers. It was the only topic that he considered to be needed by all such teachers.

Tests and measurements are used by teachers in two ways: to measure the readiness of pupils before a learning experience and to measure the achievement of pupils after they have had instruction. In the first function, measures of intellectual abilities and skills, attitudes and interests, and previous achievements are used in appraising the readiness of the pupils for some kind or level of new learning. The placement of pupils in various grade levels, or in fast or slow sections within a given grade level, is often based in part on tests. The search to understand why a pupil may not be learning to read may employ standardized tests of mental ability.

To use the results of such tests properly, teachers need to understand how the tests are made, given, and interpreted. They need to know something about how definitions of mental abilities are derived, how test questions are written and evaluated, how subtle changes in testing procedure can influence and even invalidate test results, and how the norms of mental tests are developed. They need to know something about the theory and method of estimating test reliability (the degree to which a test yields consistent measures) and especially validity (the degree to which a test score has meaning or measures what it is intended to measure). And finally, they need a background of knowledge about the results obtained in testing groups differing in age, sex, occupation, social class, urban and rural residence, and so on.

The technology of testing, especially standardized mental ability testing, is a solid achievement of the behavioral sciences in this century. Testing goes considerably beyond the commonsense folk wisdom to which Dr. Conant consigns a great deal of the content of educational psychology. This area contains a good share of the best-established content to be found in the course. Indeed, at one university the course was often begun with material on tests and measurements in an effort to gain the respectful attention of students as soon as possible.

The second major function of testing, as already noted, is to help teachers evaluate student achievement. The rationale and content in this area are also fairly well agreed upon. Teachers should know how to define the objectives of their instruction in terms of observable behavior on the part of pupils. To elicit this behavior, teachers must know how to write valid test questions. Hence prospective teachers are sensitized to the difference between test questions that elicit mere knowledge of unrelated bits of information, and questions that require higher mental processes, such as analysis, judgment, and explanation. Although not enough can be done along these lines in the first course in educational psychology, students are at least taught that the so-called objective types of test item can be used for getting at kinds of achievement other than unstructured knowledge. They are also taught that essay tests have distinct advantages when they are properly constructed and graded.

Emotional and Social Adjustment

The fourth major topic of educational psychology is emotional and social adjustment. Some books call it personality integration, the self-concept, or mental health, and it also includes such topics as character development, discipline, or social-emotional problems in the classroom. Whatever the terminology, the general area of study is clear.

Emotional and social aspects of adjustment are important not only in their own right, as objectives of child-rearing and education, but also because they determine how well pupils learn the intellectual matter that everyone agrees should be a focus of the school. During the 1930's–1950's, these emotional and social concerns of educational psychologists were strongly emphasized, but in recent years there seems to have been a countertendency to pay more attention to cognitive, intellectual aspects of learning and teaching. In any case, concern with adjustment has led to the inclusion in educational psychology of material on sociometry, group dynamics, child-centered teaching methods, counseling, role-playing, inventories of pupils' problems, and research with projective techniques.

Although in the next decade attention to these matters may be counterbalanced with emphasis on academic learning, it is unlikely that educational psychologists will cease to be deeply interested in how pupils feel and how they get along with other people. Some writers on education want to reduce to a minimum the school's concern with emotional and social matters on the ground that the school should stick to what it alone can do in our society, namely, nurture the intellect through contact with the basic academic disciplines. The home, the neighborhood, and the church should, in this view, take responsibility for character and personality development. And there has perhaps been a tendency toward this orientation during the past five or ten years. But other writers view any such tendencies with strong misgivings. They point to the millions of children in our great cities whose homes, neighborhoods, and churches—whatever ought to be their function—are not doing the job of fostering mental health and good character. And not only the dwellers in slums, the so-called culturally disadvantaged, arouse such misgivings. Newspapers carry stories of the adolescents from middle-class and wealthy homes who commit vandalism and other delinquent acts. Attempts to explain such anomalies in the behavior of children whose homes and communities seem, at least superficially, to be as good as American society affords, raise anew the question of what the schools can and should do to give students a sense of purpose and a desire to lead a good life as defined by the best in the American heritage.

In the debate on the functions of schools, most educational psychologists will be found on the side of those who want teachers to be able and willing to understand and do something constructive about the mental health and character of their pupils. Teachers are thus viewed as agents of society responsible for something more than the inculcation of the intellectual virtues. The equipment for understanding emotional and social aspects of students may not be as good as desired, and there may not exist a clear enough conception of what teachers can do with such an understanding once they have it. Nevertheless, educational psychologists for the most part are as yet unwilling to abandon the effort to give such tools and ideas to prospective teachers.

One practical consideration serves to keep such topics in the forefront of the concern of educators of prospective teachers. This is classroom discipline, which always turns up prominently in studies of the causes of failure of beginning teachers. Teachers are dismissed from their initial position most often because of failures to maintain classroom discipline and not for failures to help pupils achieve the cognitive objectives of schooling. Whatever the arguments in favor of concentrating on intellectual matters, school administrators and teachers continue to be troubled about discipline. Since discipline turns out to be a matter of emotional and social adjustment and of mental hygiene and character development, educational psychologists may be expected to continue to teach about such matters.

Determination of behavior. Underlying the approach to emotional and social adjustment that is taught to prospective teachers is a view of human behavior as caused, or determined. The working principle offered teachers is expressed in such terms as these: ". . . children generally behave in about the only way it is possible for them to behave considering the hereditary characteristics they possess, the kinds of experiences they have had, and the social pressures which are operating upon them at the moment." [6] It may be possible to argue that the child's free choice, his will power, and his self-determined character also make a difference. But most educational psychologists, at least implicitly, take the position quoted above. For it is only this position that gives the teacher, as part of the pupil's environment, any hope of influencing the pupil. The free will in pupil behavior is by definition immune from the teacher's influence. To resort to it as an explanatory principle is a counsel of despair, an admission of impotence, on the school's part.

Thus, teachers are taught to look for the causes of adjustment problems not in the pupil's intrinsic weakness, or bad character, but in the relationship between the pupil's characteristics and his environment. Misbehavior or withdrawal may result from school tasks inappropriate—too hard or too easy—to a child's abilities. The school tasks may seem to the student to be irrelevant to his needs, interests, or outlook on life. The amount of sitting still that a teacher requires may be inappropriate to a young child's need for sheer physical moving around. A teacher's behavior may seem to a student to be outrageously unfair in relation to the student's notions of legitimate teacher power.

ADJUSTMENT PROCESS

Given a concern for social and emotional adjustment, and a view of behavior as caused, what does the educational psychologist offer the prospective teacher? The answer can be built around the following model of the adjustment process that, in one form or another, has been taught for many years: adjustment begins with a need that the person then undertakes to satisfy. If his first effort to satisfy the need is frustrated, he resorts to varied kinds of behavior or to so-called adjustment mechanisms of various kinds. Eventually, the person achieves satisfaction of the need or continues to suffer frustration. In this way he builds up a kind of emotional or social adjustment.

Basic psychological needs are acquired in the process of growing up in society. There is no universally accepted scheme or list, but the following are often mentioned: status, security, affection, approval, independence, and achievement.

Under ordinary circumstances, the individual finds ways to satisfy these needs in his everyday life. He achieves the kind of status that he has come to expect. He receives the amount of affection that he has learned to need. He gains the kind of independence that seems to him appropriate to his age. He acquires the kind of self-respect he needs. His family, his peers, and his teachers in the home, neigh-

---

[6] Blair, Jones, and Simpson, *op. cit.*, p. 426.

borhood, and school interact with him in ways that leave him fairly well satisfied.

But for some persons, or on some occasions, conditions arise to frustrate such needs. It may be a personal defect or physical ailment, poverty, social customs and restrictions, conflict between competing needs, or conflict between the individual's conscience and his needs. When the individual is frustrated, he is tense, uncomfortable, rest-less—in a state of imbalance.

To reduce this frustration, he may resort to a direct and rational attack on the obstacles to the satisfaction of his needs. Or he may use one of the "adjustment mechanisms": aggression, compensation, sublimation, identification, rationalization, projection, repression, reaction formation, egocentrism, negativism, withdrawal, regression, psychosomatic ailments. He may even become neurotic or psychotic. Educational psychology courses typically deal with these adjustment mechanisms at least to the extent of defining and illustrating them. Presumably, the teacher should become able to recognize such mech-anisms in his pupils and even in his own behavior. The teacher can then cope better with the irrational ways in which his pupils some-times seek to satisfy their emotional and social needs in classroom life. Or the teacher may then be better able to recognize and fore-stall such irrationality on his own part.

DISCIPLINE

As already noted, one major aspect of concern with mental hy-giene and adjustment in school is "discipline." The term generally refers to the degree or quality of control exercised by the teacher over his pupils. Disciplinary problems are failures in such control. They take the form of all the minor and major offenses against order, the peccadilloes and crimes, that are familiar to anyone who has attended an elementary and secondary school.

Educational psychologists regard disciplinary problems as symp-toms of something wrong, rather than as the basic problems in them-selves. What to do about the specific behavior called a disciplinary problem is one thing; what to do about the underlying trouble is another. A disciplinary problem may be a symptom of something either trivial or important.

Teachers are inculcated with the principle that treating the symp-tom is not the same as solving the underlying problem. Treating the symptom may be a matter of sending the child out of the room, keeping him after school, giving him a talking to, or in some other way imposing sanctions that he will seek to avoid in the future by not repeating the kinds of behavior that caused him to have an un-pleasant experience. To determine the underlying problem, however, the teacher needs to know something about mechanisms of adjustment, behavior problems, interests and abilities, home and school environment, personality and temperament, and dynamics of social interaction in the school.

Teachers need two kinds of equipment in dealing with disciplinary problems: tactics and strategies. They need tactics to deal with the immediate problem of restoring order in the classroom and the school. They need strategies for solving the problems of emotional and social adjustment that may underlie the immediate disciplinary problem.

From this point of view, the teacher's tactics for restoring order in the classroom should be determined by whatever works in the short run and does not do harm in the long run. Such tactics, analogous to aspirin, consist of removing the disorderly pupil from the group in one way or another, or restraining him physically from continuing to misbehave, or even, in some cases, applying that universally understood measure known as corporal punishment. It does not matter too much what the teacher does as long as it works for the moment and does not do any long-range harm.

Some of the tactics that are considered to do long-range harm, in all likelihood, are punishing a whole group for the misconduct of an individual, using sarcasm or ridicule, overlooking the pupil's physical illness or disorder, or reacting to misconduct as a personal affront. In general, it is recognized as harmful to employ hard, cruel, implacable forms of punishment. Good tactics are reasonable, just, and fair; the teacher explains the reasons for the rules, allows discussion, and permits students to participate in establishing the regulations insofar as they are qualified to do so.

Educational psychologists agree fairly well on the question of punishments. For example, one book states: "Praise and social approval are more effective in promoting good standards of conduct than are censure, blame, and punishment." [7] The author of another book writes: "If one wishes merely to suppress unwanted responses during the time pupils are under the teacher's eye, consistent punishment would be expected to do the job. If the aim is to teach pupils to regulate their own conduct so that the teacher's pressure can be removed, punishment will not work." [8]

The general tone of educational psychologists is one that urges teachers to emphasize the positive kinds of reinforcement, insofar as such emphases are reasonable and workable. Given a choice between two alternative and effective ways of eliminating misbehavior, the teacher should generally choose the positive over the negative,

---

[7] *Ibid.,* p. 427.
[8] Cronbach, *op. cit.,* p. 493.

i.e., try to elicit good behavior that can be rewarded rather than merely punishing the undesirable behavior.

In social learning and imitation, the learner's model (e.g., the teacher) must be someone whom the learner likes and respects. Only when the learner positively identifies with his teacher will he be as favorably inclined as possible to adopt the teacher's attitudes and values about classroom order, among many other things. And to engender such liking and respect for their teachers on the part of students, educational psychologists advocate that, whenever a reasonable choice is at hand, the teacher give preference to reward and approval—but only when the choice is available and reasonable. Thus, the teacher ought to be alert to every opportunity to give praise and approval and to avoid reproof and punishment. But this is not the same as advocating that reproof and punishment be avoided entirely; when the need for reasonable punishment is clear and distinct, it should not go unmet.

STRATEGIES FOR FOSTERING ADJUSTMENT AND CHARACTER DEVELOPMENT

When disciplinary problems recur too often, a teacher needs to examine his strategies. Like the headache that comes back after the aspirin has worn off, a disciplinary problem may continually reappear after a tactic for handling it has run its course. Then something more than a momentary aberration is involved. Here the teacher is taught to re-examine what he knows about the readiness of his pupils for the kind of learning that he is trying to bring about. Frustration caused by repeated failure to learn or get approval, boredom resulting from a failure to see connections between what one wants and what one is required to do—such conditions indicate that a teacher's whole strategy needs re-examination if disciplinary problems are to be solved rather than merely palliated.

Educational Psychology and the Great Cities

It is in the great cities, with their large and dense concentrations of culturally deprived, lower-class families, that the problems of school adjustment and character development are especially profound. The problems are aggravated by the now well-recognized tendency of teachers to move away from positions in the big city slums, where the teaching seems harder and less rewarding.

One special aspect of big city education, accordingly, is that of teacher personnel: the recruitment, selection, education, placement, and retention of larger numbers of teachers who are better qualified for work in the great cities. It was for this reason that a research seminar on teacher education was held in June 1963 under the sponsorship of the Research Council of the Great Cities Program for School Improvement.[9] At that conference, a host of problems bearing upon such teacher education were examined, and research proposals relating to these problems were formulated. Many of the problems are not psychological ones; rather, they are administrative, financial, political, curricular, and operational.

Nonetheless, the psychological aspects of educational problems in the great cities loom extremely large. "The incidence of mental health problems is greatest in the slums. A sociologist commented that when social class figures on mental problems are examined, the only significant increase from one class to another is between the lowest socioeconomic class and the one above it." [10] The rate of school dropouts is highest in the slum areas of the big city. It is easy to defend the proposition that the best equipment of educational psychology and social work ought to be brought to bear on the problems of educating the culturally deprived child.

In concentrating on this problem, what has educational psychology to offer? As of now, its contribution would consist more of theoretical and methodological tools than of substantive findings, but even in the latter realm, some contributions have been made.[11]

In research on teacher education, the behavior and characteristics of teachers become dependent variables, while programs of teacher recruitment, selection, and training become the independent variables. In research on teaching methods, effects on pupils are the dependent variables, and teaching methods are independent variables. In research on teachers' personality, traits and characteristics are the independent variables. And finally, in research on pupils' characteristics, such characteristics of pupils as their achievement and interest in school work may be considered the dependent variables, while their social class, home environment, ethnic background, and so on, become the independent variables.

PUPIL CHARACTERISTICS

Teaching in the great cities is different because the pupils are different, particularly the pupils in the general category termed "culturally deprived." Much knowledge of the characteristics of culturally deprived children and youth is already at hand, but more is needed. Such knowledge can be categorized according to whether it deals with intellectual abilities, achievement, attitudes, interests, environment and background, emotional and social adjustment, or physical aspects.

---

[9] Great Cities Program for School Improvement, *Research Seminar on Teacher Education*, Cooperative Research Project No. G-011 (Evanston, Ill.: School of Education, Northwestern University, 1963).

[10] *Ibid.*, p. 122.

[11] Frank Riessman, *The Culturally Deprived Child* (New York: Harper & Row, 1962).

Intellectual abilities. To what degree do the test performances of culturally deprived youth reflect their environmental disadvantages, or the biases built into the tests, or indeed hereditary patterns? Research on social class and intelligence tests, recently summarized by W. W. Charters, needs to be pursued further.[12] The Davis-Eells test, intended to yield an index of problem-solving ability that was educationally significant but also fair to children from lower-class backgrounds, seems not to have succeeded well enough in eliminating social class differences or in producing scores that are valid against present-day criteria of school success.

But the search for such a test should not be abandoned. Riessman has suggested that further exploration be made of the usefulness of "games" orientations, longer time limits, fewer academic and bookish problems, methods of scoring that deal with process as well as the accuracy of the final answer, items that do not discriminate between deprived and middle-class groups, pretraining pupils in effective methods of test-taking, and training examiners in special methods of establishing rapport with culturally deprived children.

It should be recalled that in February 1964, New York City abandoned the use of group intelligence tests in its schools in favor of complete reliance on achievement tests. Teachers knowledgeable in the measurement aspects of educational psychology would at least know what questions to ask about this policy.

Educational psychology also is concerned with the organization of mental ability. Into what kinds of factors—verbal, numerical, spatial —can intelligence be analyzed? Such factors are known to exist along with a general factor of mental ability. For culturally deprived children, the question ought at least to be raised whether their mental abilities are organized factorially in the same way as those of middle-class children. That is, do they show the same results in factor analyses of mental ability as do middle-class children? Also, do batteries of mental tests have the same kind of predictive value, in regression equations, for culturally deprived children? Studies along these lines might well yield improved understanding of the cognitive processes of culturally deprived children. Such understanding might raise the validity of ability tests for such children.

Achievement of cognitive objectives. Culturally deprived youth get lower marks from teachers and lower scores on standardized achievement tests. Perhaps there are better ways of defining and appraising the achievement of culturally deprived youth; perhaps ways can be devised to help teachers eliminate their social-class biases from the

---

[12] W. W. Charters, Jr., "Social Class and Intelligence Tests," in W. W. Charters, Jr., and N. L. Gage, eds., *Readings in the Social Psychology of Education* (Boston: Allyn and Bacon, 1963), pp. 12–21.

marks and grades that they assign pupils. That such biases exist has been suggested by research on teacher's perceptions of their pupils. Studies have shown that teachers often have less favorable attitudes toward lower-class children. Pupils with a higher socioeconomic position tend to obtain higher sociometric status among their peers. If "the same factors which contribute to his rejection by peers tend to arouse attitudes of rejection on the part of the teacher," then it is readily inferred that teachers' marks tend to be biased against lower-class pupils.[13] Training teachers to understand and accept such pupils can reduce this bias in teachers' marks; similarly, curricula and objectives better suited to the needs and interests of culturally deprived pupils would reduce bias in defining and measuring educational achievement.

Attitudes, interests, and values. Riessman found that "the underprivileged person is much more oriented to the vocational, in contrast to the academic aspect of education." He has "great respect for physical science" but is "least interested in social studies, literature and the arts, as they are now presented in schools." [14] The teacher and the curriculum builder need to acquire and act upon much more detailed knowledge concerning the attitudes of culturally deprived children and youth toward different kinds of people, occupations, and activities. Careful surveys of these attitudes, obtained with inventories and open-ended questions, would allow the replacement of conjectures with facts.

Environment and background. Child-rearing practices, parent-child relationships, and cultural and physical environments determine the behavioral opportunities of children. The crowded conditions, poor sanitation, and extended family structure of the homes and neighborhoods of culturally deprived children have an influence on their strengths and limitations. Riessman offered provocative hypotheses concerning the meaning of physical punishment as used by parents of lower-class children, the possible implications of parent-child relationships in lower-class homes for the significance of psychoanalytic concepts developed by middle-class persons, and the significance for sex behavior of crowded living conditions. Again, teachers in the great cities need more detailed knowledge based on careful research.

Emotional and social adjustment. There have already been some studies of the differences between middle- and lower-class children in their responses to lists of problems to be checked if they are troublesome to the child, in their sociometric status in the classroom, in their school dropout rates, and in their morale. Teachers need better

---

[13] Norman E. Gronlund, *Sociometry in the Classroom* (New York: Harper & Brothers, 1959), p. 281.

[14] Riessman, *op. cit.,* p. 13.

knowledge in this area also, based on more careful inventories, interviews, ratings, observations, and content analyses.

The nutritional status and health problems of lower-class children need to be described and understood in relation to their schooling. Lower-class children report more health problems on checklists of their concerns and worries. The role of athletics in the life of the culturally deprived boy is different from that in the life of the suburban, middle-class son of a college-educated professional worker.

TEACHING CULTURALLY DEPRIVED CHILDREN

Teaching consists of motivating pupils, directing their perceptions, eliciting their responses, and reinforcing these responses. Some writers suggest that culturally deprived children respond best to strictly utilitarian justifications of the value of school learning. If so, the new mathematics and science curricula, intended to be less narrowly functional in everyday life, will either fail or need to be especially adapted in classes for lower-class pupils. But evidence here is scanty. Old assumptions about the futility of motivating pupils through appeals to the basic structures of mathematics and science have turned out to be false as far as middle-class pupils are concerned. It may be that a genuine effort will show these assumptions to be false for lower-class children as well, but only further research can provide an answer.

The family life of the culturally deprived child may force upon him a greater concern with sharing, co-operation, and group goals. If so, the teacher can make effective use of group processes for motivational purposes. Group projects, role-playing, team games, and incentives for group achievement may therefore prove to be more effective with lower-class children.

Methods of perception-directing. A whole school of theorists of perception has grown up around the notion that motives, needs and values exert directive influences on perceptions. Poor children have been considered to have more distorted perceptions of the sizes of coins, for example, than do rich children. The emotional significance of a word appears to influence the speed with which it can be recognized. Riessman holds that deprived children "appear to think in spatial terms rather than temporal terms (they often have poor time perspective)," and that the deprived child's style is "physical and visual rather than aural." They seem, he states, "to have a very different attitude toward abstract concepts. They need to have the abstract constantly and intimately pinned to the immediate, the sensory, the topical. This is not to say that they dislike abstract thinking. It is, rather, that they do it differently." [15]

Educational psychologists ask whether these notions—directive

---

[15] *Ibid.,* pp. 69, 73.

states in perception and differences in preferred perceptual modalities—are valid and have implications for teaching methods. These aspects of the perception-directing components of teaching seem to be worthy of investigation.

Response elicitation. Teaching can vary from the lecture method, where the learner is essentially passive, to the discussion method and programed learning, in which the learner responds frequently and actively. Research must investigate whether lower- and middle-class children differ in how well they learn under passive and active methods. Some current research on programed learning has shown that the active responding makes little difference. Children have been found to learn about as well when they read the response in the program as when they make it themselves. Yet, writers like Riessman refer to "the physical or motoric style of deprived groups." If a style exists, overt responding may be more effective in getting such children to learn. Combined with the game-like quality of teaching machines, their active response feature may make them more effective with culturally deprived children. Pupil participation in classroom processes through discussion, group planning, and other kinds of activities may also prove to be more valuable for lower-class children than middle-class children.

Reinforcement. For culturally deprived children, the value of report card grades must be questioned. If these are not meaningful, other kinds of incentives must be found. Riessman distinguished between love and respect and considered the lower-class child to want the latter particularly, since "love is not a major issue in the deprived home ... [but] respect, on the other hand, is something that the child is not likely to have received in the culture at large." [16] Teachers must be able to communicate the respect they feel, and conversely, must also gain status in the lower-class pupil's eyes. Unless the teacher has such status, he cannot be an effective dispenser of rewards. In lower-class schools, unlike middle-class schools, the teacher does not have high status automatically, but must win it.

Teachers' personalities. Teachers differ in temperament, needs, and the like. Research on the teacher's personality and characteristics has not thus far been concerned with whether various traits and characteristics have different educational significance for teachers of lower-class children than for teachers of middle-class children. Yet, in at least one instance, the validity of a teacher attitude inventory was much higher for pupils with strong affective values than for pupils with weak affective, but strong cognitive, values.[17] If lower-

16 *Ibid.,* pp. 46–47.

17 G. M. Della Piana and N. L. Gage, "Pupils' Values and the Validity of the Minnesota Teacher Attitude Inventory," *Journal of Educational Psychology,* Vol. 46, No. 3 (March 1955), pp. 167–178.

class pupils have stronger affective values concerning teachers, the attitudes measured by the Minnesota Teacher Attitude Inventory—permissive, acceptant attitudes—should be much more significant for teacher effectiveness in winning a favorable response from pupils.

Riessman has suggested that teachers of disadvantaged children should have some "identification with the underdog," should have a reformer's zeal, should be physical rather than word-ridden in their approach, and should be "dedicated." Educational psychologists would want to develop methods of measuring these dimensions and validate them against criteria of effectiveness in teacher-pupil relationships. Research on teachers' personality traits might improve if the pupils' social class is taken into account.[18]

TEACHER EDUCATION FOR THE GREAT CITIES

What is known about pupils' characteristics, teaching methods, and teachers' personalities that bears on education in the great cities should be used to improve the education of teachers for those cities. Some attempts to contend with these special problems of teacher education have already been made.[19]

Many of the teacher education problems are not, strictly speaking, problems of educational psychology. Increasing salaries, hiring more teachers to make smaller classes possible, and eliminating certain examination requirements and red tape—all these may help to improve the competitive position of the great cities in employing new teachers. Co-operative arrangements between school districts and colleges for teacher education, getting the mass media to present a better-rounded and more favorable image of what teaching in the great cities entails, and perhaps establishing special certificates for teachers of culturally deprived children have all been recommended by knowledgeable students of the problems.

Educational psychology bears not only upon the content of teacher education but also upon its methods. The best ways of teaching pupils should suggest better ways of teaching teachers. Educational psychology needs to be applied to teacher education as much as it has already been applied to the education of children in our elementary and secondary schools. Presumably, the same could be said of all kinds of professional education, including social work education.

---

[18] See J. W. Getzels and P. W. Jackson, "The Teacher's Personality and Characteristics," in N. L. Gage, ed., *Handbook of Research on Teaching* (Chicago: Rand McNally Co., 1963), pp. 506–582.

[19] See, for example, Harry N. Rivlin, "Teachers for the School in Our Big Cities" (New York: Division of Teacher Education, City University of New York, 1962) (mimeographed); Yeshiva University, Graduate School of Education, "Training Programs in Project Beacon" (New York, 1963) (mimeographed); and Great Cities Program for School Improvement, Research Council, "Teacher Education Project: Follow-up of Selected Practices" (Chicago, 1963) (mimeographed).

6

THEORIES OF
INTERPROFESSIONAL COMMUNICATION

By Erasmus L. Hoch

The thesis of the present paper is a simple one: problems of communication were not born yesterday. They are as much targets of attention as ever, but—and this will be the burden of the argument —they can now be approached from new directions with appreciable effect. If the contributions from research and theory are still far from definitive, some of the hypotheses can at least be more clearly stated, their terms operationally defined, the assumptions better recognized, and the problems more rigorously studied. Of the lines of investigation being pursued, some shall be alluded to, others explored, and a few dwelt upon in detail.

If communication seems an intractable problem, it could be because language is a tricky business. One need not flee to general semantics to prove it. It is interesting enough to note that at a simpler level English contains one or two words for snow, but Eskimo language has six or more. Whorf notes that the language people use often, in fact, directs their thinking.

> We dissect nature along lines laid down by our native languages. We cut nature up, organize it into concepts, and ascribe significances as we do, largely because we are parties to an agreement to organize it in this way—an agreement that holds throughout our speech community and is codified in the patterns of our language.[1]

For the purposes of this paper the Eskimo need not be called upon any further. Social workers, educators, psychologists, and psychia-

---

[1] B. L. Whorf, *Language, Thought and Reality* (Cambridge, Mass.: Technology Press of MIT, 1956), p. 212.

trists might in their own right provide plenty of grist for Whorf's mill.

Preliminary Considerations

Most people have come to have a healthy respect for the role *connotative* meaning plays in communication–interprofessional or otherwise. But Osgood has taken the trouble to devise a "semantic differential" for nailing down such meanings so they can be examined. By the simple expedient of having a person plot a particular word on seven-point bipolar scales, he and his collaborators have shown graphically that words do, indeed, carry different freight, for different people.[2] Thus, the characteristic profile that the word "corporation" assumes for a particular union foreman might turn out as follows:

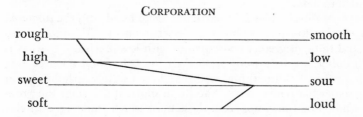

For a member of the Chamber of Commerce, for example, the word might yield a profile of quite another sort:

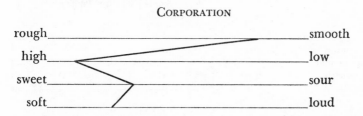

Without pursuing Osgood's explorations further, one cannot help wonder what manner of profile might be obtained from social workers and educators, not to mention psychologists and psychiatrists (and, indeed, pupils and patients), on such words as "teacher," "doctor," "problem child," "help," and "superintendent" (let alone the score of words each profession invests with extra special meanings).

---

[2] C. E. Osgood, "The Nature and Measurement of Meaning," *Psychological Bulletin*, Vol. 49, No. 3 (May 1952), pp. 197–237.

Small wonder that Osgood is elsewhere as interested, perhaps more interested, in the "real" communication problems of contemporary international relations.[3] For if interprofessional communication between education and social work (or psychology and psychiatry) poses problems of no mean magnitude, those between South Vietnam and the United States, for example, are hardly less formidable.

Wherever communication takes place, certain problems of information transmission, "channel capacities," "static," semantics, and other problems, less and more technical, are at issue. Hence, where the communication proceeds in a large organizational system with formal professional groups as partners in a joint social enterprise, it becomes someone's responsibility to look not only at the immediate perceptions and misperceptions, understandings and misunderstandings, but at the more abstract, theoretical, and research-relevant characteristics of the transaction. It is the latter that will be attended to here.

The behavioral sciences in particular seem faced with the dilemma of being able to study problems of lesser moment with great exactitude and those of greater consequence with less precision. If what is worth doing is worth doing well, then the behavioral sciences may get charged with doing things well that do not seem worth doing and doing somewhat poorly those that do. In short, at this stage the problems studied best may not seem those most worth studying, and vice versa.

Schematically, the situation is somewhat as follows:

| | | SIGNIFICANCE OF PROBLEM | |
		More	*Less*
Rigorousness of Experimental Approach	*More*	A	B
	Less	C	D

In the 2 x 2 table, A would represent the desideratum—the problem of great moment studied with great precision. By contrast, D represents the problem of little consequence that also cannot be studied well. The rub, then, seems to lie in the B's and C's of every area—those problems that are notably significant but, alas, cannot yet be handled well experimentally and/or those problems that can be investigated with great rigor but of whose value there is doubt.

Transported into the communication area and translated into so-

---

[3] C. E. Osgood, "The Psychologist in International Affairs," *American Psychologist*, Vol. 19, No. 2 (February 1964), pp. 111–118.

cial work and education terms the situation at the moment is something like the following:

SIGNIFICANCE OF PROBLEM

		More	Less
Rigorousness of Experimental Approach	More		What are the statistics regarding teachers' outside interests?
	Less	How can social work and education communicate more effectively?	

If the above can be viewed solely paradigmatically, then what needs doing is clear, although how to do it is the problem. In brief, the millennium will have arrived when the most important questions are studied with the greatest rigor. Again, schematically, the problem is to move the less/more and the more/less issues into the more/more cell, thus:

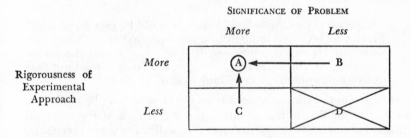

SIGNIFICANCE OF PROBLEM

Box A is the desideratum—the area in which what is done well is also worth doing. Box D, by contrast, is of little concern, if any. How to make A's out of B's and C's—that is the question; and whether it is better to work from practice toward theory or the other way around is something else again. The present conference fortunately sees merit in both.

Theoretical Approaches

One need hardly be reminded that communication problems are not unique to those among professions. Communications satellites symbolize no mean accomplishment, telemetry enables scientists to watch the heartbeat of astronauts at 18,000 per hour and 1,500 miles away, and United Nations interpreters try to catch the turn of every phrase lest faulty communication invite disaster.

One might suggest, therefore, that communication is all of a piece, that interprofessional communication is part of a much larger theoretical whole, and that, if professions can afford the time and the patience, they have much to gain from looking at how people in many quarters are studying communication and what they are finding out. There they will find a variety of specialists talking about a great big system in which communication is taking place for better or worse, information is getting exchanged well or poorly, a certain amount of "gaming" is going on, and, all in all, attitudes are getting changed in the process.

There are four theoretical approaches to the problem of communication, each of which is trying in its way to bring order out of chaos: systems theory, communication and information theory, game and decision theory, and models of attitude change. Each of them, in its present form, is relatively young and none of them presumes to have settled the problems at this stage; all of them proceed with vigor —and hope—nonetheless.

GENERAL BEHAVIOR SYSTEMS THEORY

> Some twenty or thirty years hence, it could be that social scientists will be using standardized concepts and terms which, today, are strange or unknown. It is likely, too, that the future language of the social sciences often will be cast in a form that electronic computers can "understand" and use.[4]

McClelland's estimate of twenty or thirty years may be optimistic or pessimistic depending on how a profession feels at the moment. But in light of the feats of this decade, its realization seems inevitable. General systems theory will see to that.

When Maxwell Jones made the psychiatric world aware that a hospital is but part of a larger "therapeutic community," he caused many to take a second look at what was happening to patients on their wards.[5] When the System Development Corporation is as interested in school systems as in the giant communication networks of national defense, it opens other eyes as widely. In working toward more effective interprofessional communication, then, it is necessary to keep constantly in view the larger context in which social work and education speak to each other.

---

[4] C. A. McClelland, "General Systems and the Social Sciences," *Etc.*, Vol. 18, No. 4 (February 1962), pp. 449–468.

[5] M. Jones, *The Therapeutic Community* (New York: Basic Books, 1953).

General systems theory is concerned with processes that involve everything from subatomic particles to galaxies. General behavior systems theory, a subcategory concerned with living systems, tailors the problem a bit more to size as it limits itself to the range from virus to cell to organ to individual to small group to society. There are enough lessons there to be learned.

The research of Stanton and Schwartz has vividly demonstrated that when a psychiatric patient suddenly renews the wetting and soiling he had stopped three months ago, the explanation may lie less in anal complexes than in the fact that the social worker and the doctor are fighting about smoking in the mess hall. By the same token, systems theorists would suggest, the solution does not lie in having the psychiatrist overrule or accede to the social worker (or in having each seek the support of the nurse and psychologist). Rather, it involves getting both to realize that how the two of them communicate has implications for many people—more theoretically, that their behavior takes place in a large open system.[6]

Though Stanton and Schwartz did not couch their conclusions in systems theory terminology, their very real-life investigations of a psychiatric hospital could well be so formulated. The systems theorist might describe the phenomena in his own way: "When inputs or loads create strains great enough to call into play complex subsystems to restore equilibrium, we sometimes refer to such processes as 'defense mechanisms.' " [7] Phraseology aside, however, he would hasten to point out that when the visiting social worker and the school principal interact, the results of the communication go much beyond the two parties; that when committees of the National Association of Social Workers and the National Education Association exchange (and later publish) ideas about mental health in the schools, the information makes its way into other systems in the form of various inputs and results in various outputs; that when Dr. Conant makes recommendations, both professional organizations (and others) receive an input that each system handles in its own way.[8]

General behavior systems theory hardly promises that all communication problems will suddenly be solved if talk about "professions" and "disciplines" gives way to talk about "systems." But it does say there must be a newer and better way of writing out some of the rules of the game. If the profession of social work is a dynamic,

---

[6] A. H. Stanton and M. S. Schwartz, *The Mental Hospital* (New York: Basic Books, 1954).

[7] J. G. Miller, "Toward a General Theory for the Behavioral Sciences," *American Psychologist*, Vol. 10, No. 9 (September 1955), pp. 513–531.

[8] *See* James B. Conant, *The Education of American Teachers* (New York: McGraw-Hill Book Co., 1963).

living, open system in operation rather than an aggregation of social workers, how does it handle such inputs as the final report of the Joint Commission on Mental Illness and Health? [9] How does President Johnson's signing of the education bill affect the subsequent communication patterns between education and social work? What processes take place within each system as it interacts with the other? Can results be specified when certain inputs (of information, rumor, suggestion, and the like) enter the system? Can the strains in a profession be detected and their effects studied in system-relevant terms?

Systems theory is not simply calling the rose by another name. It is, rather, looking at the functions of stamen and pistil, how roses bud, bloom, and fade, in what soil they best thrive, and to what blights they fall prey. It is interested in specifying how the way in which the National Education Association and the American Council on Education view the National Defense Education Act affects the exchange of information between the two. It would like to provide a scientific basis for assessing how the mushroom growth of one subsystem—clinical psychology—affects the functioning of the larger system of psychology, and how that system in turn interacts with the system labeled psychiatry. It is interested in arriving at principles that may some day, for example, help predict in advance how a statute requiring school social workers to have two years of teaching experience would affect communication patterns between a state council of social workers and a state department of education.

Is it too much to hope that when technology has advanced to the point where one can spot a burned-out fuse in a missile on its way to the moon, one might be able to develop a scientific analysis of the processes, phenomena, and parameters of interprofessional communication? The systems theorist would hardly see the task as insuperable.

COMMUNICATION AND INFORMATION THEORY

Unfortunately, much of the language of communications theorists smacks enough of mathematics and engineering to scare off the less hardy and obscure the relevance of their body of theory for the processes that go on when people (or groups) communicate. Represented symbolically and with a minimum of technical jargon, the communication process seems slightly less awesome and considerably more relevant to communication of whatever sort. [10]

---

[9] Joint Commission on Mental Illness and Health, *Action for Mental Health* (New York: Basic Books, 1961).

[10] *See*, C. E. Shannon, *The Mathematical Theory of Communication* (Urbana; University of Illinois Press, 1949).

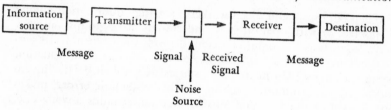

Put in simplest terms, the communication process, as Weaver categorized it, presents some straightforward questions on several levels:

Level A. How accurately can the symbols of communication be transmitted? (The technical problem)

Level B. How precisely do the transmitted symbols convey the desired meaning? (The semantic problem)

Level C. How effectively does the received meaning affect conduct in the desired way? (The effectiveness problem) [11]

It turns out that what happens at Level A bears a relationship to what goes on at Levels B and C. When information gets exchanged between NASW and the U.S. Office of Education, for example, how much "noise" (i.e., static) is there in the communication system? Anyone who has tried to watch a telecast through "snow" on a television screen, will agree that such "noise" interferes with transmission and reception, distorting the message in the process.

Communication and information theorists do not expect that to be news. They do, however, expect that one can specify "laws" concerning the exchange of information much as the physicist has already specified them for the exchange of heat and energy. Rapoport, for instance, suggests that there is little difficulty in reading the following, in which, as the message states, 25 percent of the letters have been deleted at random:

FR EXMPLE WENTYIVE PRCET OF HE LTTERS I TIS SENTENCE HVEBEN DLETED AT RANM.[12]

"It is reasonable to ask why we are so redundant," Miller admits. "The answer lies in the fact that redundancy is an insurance against mistakes. . . . The large amount of redundancy that we seem to insist on reflects our basic inefficiency as information-handling systems." [13]

---

[11] W. Weaver, "Recent Contributions to the Mathematical Theory of Communication," *Etc.*, Vol. 10, No. 4 (Summer 1953), pp. 261–281.

[12] A. Rapoport, "What Is Information?" *Etc.*, Vol. 10, No. 4 (Summer 1953), p. 257.

[13] G. A. Miller, "What Is Information Measurement?" *American Psychologist*, Vol. 8, No. 1 (January 1953), p. 8.

When educators and social workers exchange information among themselves or with each other, as individuals or as groups, on what basis, according to communication theory, might such factors as "redundancy," "bias," and others enter to affect the information being exchanged? On many bases, suggests Campbell.[14] His "inventory of biases," containing the sources of "systematic error," makes one marvel at the fact that anyone ever understands anyone else. In its transmission, information can get abbreviated, condensed, appreciably less detailed, arbitrarily categorized. It can be distorted to please the receiver or heard in terms of messages the receiver expects to hear; some of the information can be selectively attended to, some of it filtered out.

GAME THEORY AND DECISION-MAKING

Everything that passes between professions is not invariably sweetness and light. Sometimes, when all is said and done, the communication seems to have involved an element of sizing up one's opposite number and even a jockeying for position. One class of theorists has felt it eminently worthwhile to look frankly at such transactions (between parties other than education and social work) in the hope that a systematic analysis of "gaming" might lead to a closer understanding of how decisions of many kinds get made.

The classic dilemma of the prisoner recalls the seamier side of interprofessional communication. Two suspects are apprehended by the police, taken to jail, and placed in separate cells, so that communication between them is not possible. The authorities are sure the two are guilty of a certain crime but need some additional evidence. Accordingly, they tell each separately that there are certain alternatives. If neither confesses, they will each be booked on some lesser charge and given the corresponding punishment. If both confess, they will be prosecuted, but with the recommendation of a lesser sentence than normally attaches to the crime they have committed. If one confesses and the other does not, the former will receive a comparatively light sentence, the latter the stiffest possible.

The game and decision theorists are less interested in the prisoners than in the dilemma—in the factors that combine to shape a decision. To be sure, the situation need hardly be so hypothetical. Psychologists and psychiatrists, for example, have occasionally played the game without calling it by technical names (perhaps even without realizing it). Thus, everyone agrees mental health needs are great, mental health personnel is scarce, and graduate programs do not promise to correct the professional manpower shortage in the

_____
[14] D. T. Campbell, "Systematic Error on the Part of Human Links in Communications Systems," *Information and Control*, Vol. 1, No. 4 (December 1958), pp. 334–369.

near future. The prisoners in *this* case are asking themselves such questions as the following: How will certification laws affect the psychologist-psychiatrist balance in private practice? Should nurses be trained to do psychotherapy? Is group practice a boon or a bane? How will chemotherapy affect the future of psychotherapy? Whether verbalized or not, such considerations will enter into the "moves" made by a profession and its members as well as shape the decisions made as a result of, or in the absence of, interprofessional communication.

Game theory has been mentioned not as representative of a sophisticated approach to the strategy of insuring one's position, but rather as a theoretical attempt to throw some light on just what is involved when groups and their representatives try to find their place in a hierarchy vis-à-vis each other. There is a certain element of "gaming" in whether the teacher or the principal shall refer a pupil to the social worker; in setting up required courses that a group in one profession feels are "good" for another; in deciding which profession shall administer the pupil personnel services in a given school system. The problems can be talked out, doubtless to good advantage. They can also be investigated more systematically, so that their theoretical bases become clearer, in the hope that the general principles that may emerge will have applicability far beyond any immediate, specific situation.

In a fascinating extension of game theory, Meier and his students have actually had groups play out twenty years of history during less than twenty hours of gaming.[15] His "Metropolis" game, in which participants take such roles as politician, speculator, administrator and planner, each investing chips in an attempt to optimize a hypothetical city's growth potential, allows some uncanny insights into the vicissitudes of intergroup co-operation and competition. In another version, in which the balance of nature in wildlife is gamed by a group of players representing moose, beaver, and wolf, considerable theoretical understanding of the balance of nature has accrued as a result. In a wild moment of speculation, one might be tempted to cast psychiatrist, psychologist, and social worker in analogous roles to see whether one could play out that kind of relationship, the better to understand it.

MODELS OF ATTITUDE CHANGE

When C. P. Snow spoke of his "two cultures," he hardly meant social work and education:

---

[15] R. L. Meier, "Progress Report on Simulation of Ecological Relationships." Address before the Mental Health Research Institute, University of Michigan, March 19, 1964.

For constantly I felt I was moving among two groups—comparable in intelligence, identical in race, not grossly different in social origin, earning about the same incomes, who had almost ceased to communicate at all, who in intellectual, moral and psychological climate had so little in common that instead of going from Burlington House or South Kensington to Chelsea, one might have crossed an ocean.[16]

But his pointed observations regarding the particular "gulf of mutual incomprehension" should make any two groups want to be doubly sure they do not ". . . have a curious distorted image of each other." Where the latter proves to be the case, communication is doubtless a necessary, if not sufficient, condition for attitude change.

Snow is interested in why people view each other as they do, and how they can do something about it. Those who, in armchairs or laboratories, are developing "models of attitude change" share his concern. They choose to do on a more theoretical level what others are attempting on a level closer to "reality." In spite of that, or because of it, it is worth listening for a few moments to what these theoretically oriented colleagues have to say.

They suggest frankly that one might make so bold as to "scale" attitudes of person toward person, group toward group, or person and group toward Issue X, much as intelligence has been scaled. Thurstone and others have, in fact, not shrunk from scaling attitudes toward disarmament, labor unions, and political parties. It would not seem harder to do so with attitudes toward other professions or the professional leaders in one's own.[17]

As one group of models charts it, one person's political preferences may look something like the following:

$$+3 \;—\; \phi \; \text{Goldwater}$$
$$+2 \;—\; \phi \; \text{Romney}$$
$$+1 \;—\; \phi \; \text{Nixon}$$
$$0 \;—\; \phi \; \text{Lodge}$$
$$-1 \;—\; \phi \; \text{Rockefeller}$$
$$-2 \;—\; \phi \; \text{Johnson}$$
$$-3 \;—\; \phi \; \text{Humphrey}$$

---

[16] C. P. Snow, *The Two Cultures and the Scientific Revolution* (New York: Cambridge University Press, 1959), pp. 2–3.

[17] *See* L. L. Thurstone and E. J. Chave, *The Measurement of Attitudes* (Chicago: University of Chicago Press, 1929).

Another's may look like this:

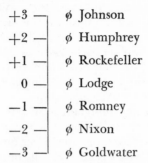

To suggest that the same device might be used to compare attitudes toward superintendents, principals, social work supervisors, and parents, might not be the most far-fetched idea one could come up with. And to suggest that such devices might, by the same token, help measure changes in attitude (hopefully in the "right" direction as the result of improved interprofessional communication) might be equally tolerable.

Other model-builders, concerned with "balance theory," have turned their theoretical talents to looking for clearer insights into how seemingly irreconcilable attitudes are reconciled. Confronted with the following situation for example, an attitudinal "imbalance" is experienced that somehow demands rectification:

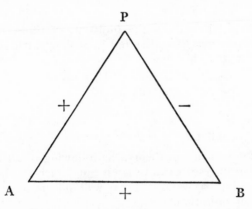

P likes the school principal (A), sees the school social worker (B) as an intruder, but learns to his dismay that the principal and the social worker have a fine professional relationship with each other.

It might be profitable to visualize oneself as P in some typical situations faced every day in social work or education. There will be little trouble imagining A's and B's who stand in various relationships to each other and, depending upon how they are viewed, cause varying degrees of balance or imbalance. Whoever has lingering doubts about the real life applicability of such theorizing will be reassured by a look at Newcomb's detailed study of the relationships that evolved among two successive groups of seventeen dormitory students in the course of their acquaintance process.[18]

When people and professions communicate, the transaction goes quite beyond the simple exchange of information. Incoming messages have a way of being consonant or dissonant in relation to perceptions a person or group holds. When incoming information is dissonant, Festinger suggests, or when a person's behavior in a situation is not consonant with his general self-concept, he has to handle somehow the cognitive discrepancy. Indeed, Festinger sees the reduction or elimination of cognitive dissonance as being as dominant a motive as the satisfaction of hunger.

All of the foregoing is presented for what it frankly represents— honest attempts on the part of capable theorists to spin the best theory or build the best model they can at this time. The common quest is a set of general principles of wide applicability that will help account for and promote understanding of the relations of men and groups.

Many roads lead to this same Rome; there are certainly other routes to travel and one might well converge on the same goal from different directions. Research is one road.

Research

Much research of relevance to the problems of interprofessional communication is in progress. Past and present research efforts can be arrayed under three headings:

1. Attempts at conceptualization of the problem
2. Data-gathering and assessment efforts
   a. Surveys
   b. Field studies
3. Laboratory simulation of real-life processes

Again, as in the discussion of theory, the following is not intended as a pocket digest of research in progress but rather as a brief look at representative investigations that may well aid the cause of interprofessional communication.

ATTEMPTS AT CONCEPTUALIZATION

While some have plunged precipitately into concrete problems of interprofessional relations, others have made haste more slowly.

---

[18] T. M. Newcomb, *The Acquaintance Process* (New York: Holt, Rinehart & Winston, 1961).

Merton has given considerable thought to what is going on in certain professions but he has been even more concerned with what is going on in professions generally.[19] His "sociology of the professions" demonstrates that there is merit in laying aside the professional problems of the moment in order to think about the general direction of the professions. The Joint Commission on Mental Illness and Health has, in its own way, been doing the same thing. Its concern has been less with the immediate problem of curing people than with a kaleidoscopic conception of what the whole field of mental health entails.

Table 1 gives an example of a science and profession trying to conceptualize the forces that shape its character. Prepared by the Committee on Scientific and Professional Responsibility of the American Psychological Association, the table shows the 156 different ways in which psychologists and psychology are influenced.[20]

Space does not allow illustrations of the kind of observations the committee wrote into each of the cells. But a quick look down Column 2 (Teaching), for example, readily discloses that where it intersects with Rows 2, 3, 4, 5, 13, 14, and 16 psychology, social work, and education are constantly rubbing elbows with greater or less effectiveness. The committee report points out the following:

> One of the most pervasive problems of all professions (and of science) is a romantic myth of the professional as a lone knight on a white charger jousting an intellectual problem, or fighting a client's cause. In practice he turns out to be a working member of a group, receiving a salary or a fee, and doing a lot of things that simply cannot be done from the back of a horse.[21]

Another example of an attempt by the American Psychological Association to conceptualize interprofessional relations is the study entitled *Psychology and Its Relations with Other Professions*. Of its thirteen "aspirations for the good profession," at least two bear on the present conference.

> A good profession will maintain good channels of communication among the "discoverers," the teachers, and the appliers of knowledge.

---

[19] *See,* for example, Robert K. Merton, "Issues in the Growth of a Profession," address given before the American Nurses Association, Atlantic City, N.J., June 10, 1953; and "Some Thoughts on the Professions in American Society," address given at commencement, Brown University, Providence, R.I., June 6, 1960.

[20] *See* R. A. Bauer, *et al.,* "Social Influences on the Standards of Psychologists," *American Psychologist,* Vol. 19, No. 3 (March 1964), pp. 167–173.

[21] *Ibid.,* p. 171.

TABLE 1. INFLUENCES ACTING ON PSYCHOLOGISTS IN THE SIX AREAS OF PSYCHOLOGICAL FUNCTION

Influences	Basic and Applied Research	Teaching	Service to Client and Employer	Public Service	Professional Relations	Writing, Publishing, Speaking
Interpersonal influences						
1. Peers						
2. Members of related professions						
3. Clients, employers, and students						
4. Teachers						
5. Superiors and subordinates						
6. Editors						
7. Fund-granting agencies						
8. The public						
Group membership influences						
9. Psychological associations						
10. Private professional organizations						
11. Scientific societies (AAAS, etc.)						
12. Honorary societies						
13. Training institutions and departments						
14. Organizations where psychologists work						
Formal social regulatory influences						
15. University admission and degree requirements						
16. Certifying and licensing legislation						
17. American Board of Examiners in Professional Psychology						
18. Education and Training Board certification						
19. Code of ethics						
20. Grievance committees						
Other influences						
21. Employment standards						
22. Published occupational descriptions						
23. Security standards						
24. Standards for telephone listing						
25. Standards for malpractice insurance						
26. Awards						

A good profession will engage in rational and cooperative relations with other professions having related or overlapping competences and common purposes. . . . When related professions forget their common goals and concentrate on superficial points of conflict, a tendency that is sometimes facilitated by the existence of professional organizations, defenses are up, rationality is down, and maladaptive behavior is the result.[22]

DATA-GATHERING AND ASSESSMENT

Social workers, educators, and psychologists have hardly been remiss in looking at intra- and interprofessional problems.[23] The study by Zander and his colleagues of a group of professions in terms of their mutual perceptions and beliefs is typical.[24] Examining the writings of members of the mental health professions and conducting pilot interviews with psychiatrists, clinical psychologists, and psychiatric social workers provided first-hand insights into how beliefs and mutual perceptions are related to a profession's role, status, and power.

Elsewhere, Zander has reported some findings of his group based on two-hour interviews with a sample of individuals in the same three professions from eight different kinds of institutions in six major American cities. Such direct investigation allows conclusions that, in the absence of data, would remain only conjectures. For example:

> We have seen that in general the psychologists and social workers react similarly to the psychiatrists' higher status. They desire more support from the psychiatrists, are more supportive and cautious in their communication to them, place more value on psychiatry than the psychiatrists place on social work and psychology, and find the psychiatrists more threatening than the psychiatrists find them.[25]

But psychologists and social workers cannot so easily be lumped together, the investigators point out.

---

[22] American Psychological Association, *Psychology and Its Relations with Other Professions* (Washington, D.C., 1954), pp. 6–7.

[23] *See,* for example, Arlien Johnson, *School Social Work—Its Contribution to Professional Education* (New York: National Association of Social Workers, 1962); Educational Policies Commission, National Education Association, *The Central Purpose of American Education* (Washington, D.C.: National Education Association, 1961); and A. Roe, *et al., Graduate Education in Psychology* (Washington, D.C.: American Psychological Association, 1959).

[24] A. Zander, A. R. Cohen, and E. Stotland, *Role Relations in the Mental Health Professions* (Ann Arbor, Mich.: Institute for Social Research, 1957).

[25] A. Zander, A. R. Cohen, and E. Stotland, "Power and the Relations Among Professions," in D. Cartwright, ed., *Studies in Social Power* (Ann Arbor, Mich.: Research Center for Group Dynamics, Institute for Social Research, 1959), p. 28.

While the two adjunct groups do reveal highly similar responses to the superior status of psychiatrists, psychologists appear to have a stronger desire for equality and to react more strongly to the psychiatrists' superiority.

Nor are the psychiatrists all of a piece, for that matter: The psychiatrist with high power feels that he is admired and respected, wishes to have frequent professional contacts with subordinates, assumes that they are interested in his good will, and thinks well of their competence. The psychiatrist with low power thinks less well of the ancillary group members, assumes that they are attempting to invade his professional prerogatives rather than win his support, and thinks poorly of their competence.[26]

Certainly educators as a group have not disdained surveys either. Indeed, when Dr. Conant reports them, they get more than the quota of attention ordinarily accorded survey results.[27] If those of the National Education Association and the American Council on Education do not have the same detonating effect, they yield, nevertheless, considerable grist for the mill of interprofessional communication.

This discussion suggests that improved interprofessional communication rests upon the gathering of such facts, but that there is, at the same time, need of some master taxonomers who can lay out the data in a conceptual matrix that will yield the theoretical understanding of professional relations in a way that immersion in day-to-day problems cannot.

If surveys are half the research picture, field studies are the other. The analysis by Cogswell and Bushnell of the pupil personnel data-processing functions of a Southern California school district shows that even such large enterprises as the System Development Corporation are showing interest in the problems.[28]

Perhaps the prime current example, however, is one of the most recent—the Interprofessional Research Commission on Pupil Personnel Services.[29] Supported by the National Institute of Mental

---

26 *Ibid.*, pp. 28, 34.

27 James B. Conant, *The American High School Today* (New York: McGraw-Hill, 1959).

28 J. F. Cogswell and D. D. Bushnell, *Report of a Preliminary Analysis of the Counseling and Pupil Personnel Data Processing Functions of a Southern California School District* ("TM (L) Series No. 655"; Santa Monica, Calif.: System Development Corporation, 1961).

29 Erasmus L. Hoch, "The Interprofessional Research Commission on Pupil Personnel Services," *Psychology in the Schools*, Vol. 1, No. 1 (January 1964), pp. 27–30.

Health (after an initial assist from the U. S. Office of Education), the commission of fifteen national professional and educational associations is in the early stages of a five-year program of research and demonstration that will involve interprofessional communication on the broadest scale.

The primary purpose of the commission is to promote "a combined effort of the responsible parties to design, develop, and interpret on a national scale a program of research and demonstration in the area of pupil personnel services with the aim of providing more effective educational services for all children and youth." The broad-gauged exercise in interprofessional communication that the commission's program necessarily entails represents a story with three morals:

1. Problems of interprofessional communication become most apparent when information exchange takes place in open discussion among several professions around common objectives.

2. The improvement in interprofessional communication is less a solution to problems as such than a subject on which research needs to be done.

3. As Sherif found in his field study of co-operation and conflict among boys in a summer camp: "cooperation between groups as a consequence of interaction in situations embodying superordinate goals has a cumulative effect in the direction of reducing existing tensions between them." [30]

The Interprofessional Research Commission on Pupil Personnel Services involves just such a superordinate goal. The commission numbers among its member organizations the American Association of School Administrators, the Association for Supervision and Curriculum Development, the Council for Exceptional Children, and other education organizations, including the National Education Association itself; at the same time it embraces the National Association of Social Workers, the American Psychiatric Association, the American Medical Association, and others of the pupil personnel services family. If four regional research and demonstration centers, a commission of fifteen national associations, and the respective professions represented spell interprofessional communication on a mass scale, then here may well be a Mecca to which investigators of the phenomena may wish to repair during the next few years.

SIMULATION OF REAL-LIFE PROCESSES

Interprofessional communication can only prove the loser unless, like Janus, the field looks two ways at once. For what a little while

---

[30] M. Sherif, *et al., Intergroup Conflict and Cooperation: The Robbers Cave Experiment* (Norman, Okla.: University Book Exchange, 1961), p. 196.

ago seemed science fiction has turned out to have a reality of its own. The "automated" approach to current problems in general and computer simulation in particular has arrived. There are real lessons to be learned here for professional relations as a whole and for inter-professional communication as an aspect thereof.

Whoever doubts that the new technologies have arrived, not only in national defense and space flight but in education and social work as well, need but look at a typical article by Cogswell.[31] He finds it not too hard to bridge the gap between the man-machine systems of large military networks and the application of the "systems approach" to the counseling function of the school. While the three days spent by the investigators collecting data in a school system were not intended as evaluation of the particular system, they yielded plenty of hypotheses about how school systems and the people running them might better be studied.

To illustrate with just one of the several findings, expressed in systems language:

> The interaction between various subsystems was weak. Information that could be of use to the teaching subsystem was collected and stored in the counseling subsystem and information collected for the counseling subsystem could have been more easily collected in the teaching subsystem and transmitted to the counseling subsystem. The flow of information between the two subsystems was minimal. Channels for the transmission of information were not well established.[32]

If someone were to say that the researchers are simply stating in fancy language what others have noted and reported in the *lingua franca* of the educational world, no one would argue the point. What is different, however, is that the investigators are seeking new ways to generate and test the most pertinent hypotheses their heuristic efforts yield. Their "automated diagnostic interview of student learning behavior" will doubtless gain the attention (if not raise the hackles) of both social workers and educators (and counselors, and psychologists, and others).

> A computer-controlled teaching system could be used to simulate the adaptive questioning of the skilled interviewer. When the students' responses to questions indicate a problem area, the system would explore the area in depth. The students' responses during the interview would be recorded automatically. Almost immediately following the interview, individualized reports would be available for each student.[33]

---

[31] J. F. Cogswell, *The Systems Approach as a Heuristic Method in Educational Development—An Application to the Counseling Function* ("SP Series No. 720"; Santa Monica, Calif.: System Development Corporation, 1962).

[32] *Ibid.*, p. 4.

[33] *Ibid.*, p. 7.

The technological implementation of such notions is already more than a gleam in someone's eye. It takes one full page of Cogswell's article, for example, to diagram the computerization of how students might possibly respond to a single interview item, namely: "When you are presented with difficult problems to solve in class or in homework, do you first work on the easy items before you do the more difficult problems?" Depending upon the sequence of student responses to this particular item, the computer would print out such diagnostic assessments as the following:

1. Although not of low ability, student turns to teacher for help when faced with difficult problems rather than try to solve them.

2. Shows defensive reaction to difficult problems. Rejects the stressful situation, rather than apply effort to solution by trying or getting help.

3. Although cares for schoolwork, does not attempt to solve difficult problems and this does not bother him.[34]

Is this interprofessional communication at work? In its unique way, yes. "The hypotheses that were discussed focused primarily upon strengthening the interaction between the counseling and teaching functions," says Cogswell. If the professions are willing to think in these terms, they may be able to learn much about the business of intercommunication, even if they learn only that there is nothing here to be learned.

In actual fact, neither social work nor education nor psychology nor any of their fellow disciplines can stay the tide, even if they should want to; the collection of articles in Borko's compendium of computer applications in the behavioral sciences will attest to that.[35] The computer is humming away in medicine and neurology, in industry and language laboratories, in the composer's chamber and in the area of international relations. Interprofessional communication in its broadest sense is everywhere at issue.

To the objection that computer processes are not "real," the specialists retort they are in a sense more real in allowing one to turn back the clock in order to replay history a second time (or even a third or a fourth). As Rome and Rome put it:

> Now with the computer, something impossible in real life can be done. In real life, neither real biological nor real social organisms can ever repeat their history in any literal sense. Organic life is inherently developmental. With the computer, we do simulate such development with considerable sophistication. . . . We can plan investigations with the computer

34 *Ibid.*, p. 9.

35 H. Borko, ed., *Computer Applications in the Behavioral Sciences* (Englewood Cliffs, N.J.: Prentice-Hall, 1962).

programs in which every feature will remain the same in successive runs except one pervasive feature. . . . By this process, using the computer as a synthesizer of a total system, we can factor out the effects of a particular aspect of system operations in large social organizations.[36]

In the world of everyday communication, however, the professions and their members cannot really replay any of their transactions to see what would have happened if information had been communicated or withheld in a different way. Even a role-playing situation, for all its laboratory usefulness, is different the second time because its participants have been changed by the first go-round. The opportunity to tinker with communication patterns would be most welcome, but the urgency of ongoing professional transactions leaves little room for experimentation. The computer has many more degrees of freedom and goes about its job with enviable precision to boot. As the same authors point out:

. . . the computer does not tolerate ambiguity. Any realization is formal and precise—utter precision is guaranteed by computer realization. We conclude that if we can realize an abstract general analog of a social organization in a computer, then we realize more than the mere formal essence of any one social organization. . . . A general purpose computer is converted into a laboratory instrument of great power for investigating many kinds of social relationships in large productive social groups. What results is an elaborate engine for determining the consequence of theories of an intermediate level between real life and the most general theory of social process.[37]

Peroration

Much of the foregoing may well have made it seem that the theoretical camel was, indeed, poking its nose under the professional tent. But if some of the current research and theory affront customary ways of working toward improved professional relations, it is well sometimes to countenance the seemingly implausible.

Professional roles can be imaginative or stereotyped. Education, social work, and psychology are philosophies and ways of life as much as they are bodies of knowledge and sets of functions. In the press of circumstance, it is easy to grab the same old hat that has served so well. There may well be others to try on for size, some of which might be as flattering, and perhaps even wear better.

---

[36] S. C. Rome and B. K. Rome, "Computer Simulation Toward a Theory of Large Organizations," in Borko, ed., *op. cit.*, p. 553.

[37] *Ibid.*, pp. 553–554.

One that might be worn more often and more comfortably is that of social scientist, observer of the passing scene as well as participant in it. It is easy to get caught up in a movement, harder to collect data on it. It is easier for the professor to teach his subject than to back off from it to look at his teaching technique. The worker in a social work agency is more prone to react to the pronouncements of the new administrator than to ask what it is he might be trying to prove. The school principal is tempted to settle an argument between his social worker and nurse rather than view the situation as data to be collected if his school is to be better understood.

In a sense, this Conference on Interprofessional Communication amounts to such a bringing together of data. Indeed, there would be nothing to discuss rationally if the participants had not decided a while ago to think about the problems of interprofessional communication rather than to remain helplessly caught up in them. Much of the discussion is, in effect, about the data in the form of "critical incidents"—empirical fragments that would have gotten lost had not some participants stepped back from this or that interprofessional exchange (at the time or later) to observe what was or had been happening.

This is not to imply that somewhere answers lie that, once grasped, will forever have laid the questions to rest. The price of good interprofessional communication is eternal vigilance. As Norbert Wiener writes: "The idea that information can be stored in a changing world without an overwhelming depreciation in its value is false. . . . Information is more a matter of process than of storage." [38]

It is of this same process that the 1962 Yearbook of the Association for Supervision and Curriculum Development speaks:

> One of the great handicaps to progress in human institutions is the lag which often exists between the production of new ideas in the learned disciplines and their expression in our social institutions. It sometimes happens that many years may pass before a new idea discovered in the laboratory or formulated in theory finds its way into the daily operations of human practice.[39]

Perhaps the present conference may, if it seems wise, do a bit about that.

---

[38] *The Human Use of Human Beings* (Boston: Houghton Mifflin Company, 1950), pp. 120–121.

[39] Association for Supervision and Curriculum Development, *Perceiving, Behaving, Becoming,* Yearbook of the Association (Washington, D.C., 1962), p. 3.

part II

THE CONFERENCE

7

AN ACCOUNT OF
THE CONFERENCE DISCUSSION

By Robert H. Beck

Values, Objectives, and Functions of Social Work

Two papers prepared for the conference, "The Social Work Profession" by Werner W. Boehm and "Education of Social Workers" by Ruth E. Smalley, discuss in depth the values and goals of the social work profession.[1] These papers provided a frame of reference for conference discussion in the area of the profession's values, objectives, and functions. The impressive agreement of social workers on professional preparation and goals is clearly indicated by the concepts presented by these authors and by the general acceptance of these concepts by the conference's social work participants.

VALUES ESTEEMED BY THE SOCIAL WORK PROFESSION

Social work is committed to two chief values, one personal and individual, the other social. The one seeks the good of the individual; the other looks to the good of society. These two "goods" are compatible. They rest on the concept that society is best served if men create and have an evironment in which they are free and in which they find the means to be educated, to be employed, and to live beyond a subsistence level. Social work must attack the subsistence problems of modern life, which Boehm characterizes as "instrumental or survival problems." It must also be concerned with noninstrumental, aspirational problems and other problems that appear in the

---

[1] *See* pp. 11–30 and pp. 49–66.

guise of apathy, lack of individuality, inarticulateness, intellectual conformity, or insensitivity. The drive of social work appears to come from allegiance to these twin values—subsistence and self-fulfillment.

At no point in the discussion was there a suggestion that the social work profession has a monopoly on the goal of creating a society that would permit men both to subsist and to fulfill themselves. On the contrary, discussion brought out clearly social work's desire to work with education and all the "helping professions." This rejection of insularity made possible an approach to the concept of interprofessional communication within the framework of the community.

OBJECTIVES OF SOCIAL WORK

The objectives of social work were categorized by Boehm as social habilitation and social restoration. There was consensus that these two objectives were accepted by the social work profession and were welded into the philosophy of most social workers. However, no group of social workers is exclusively concerned with social habilitation while another group is similarly concerned with social restoration. Since its beginning, the profession has sought to keep these two objectives cemented together; today they are interdigitated. This means that no wing of social work presses for the remedy of social pathology through the reconstruction of society—a reasonably strong statement of social habilitation—while another wing strains for help available for giving material relief, family care, and related services. A summary of what is involved in carrying out these two purposes, based on the conference papers and discussions, follows.

Social habilitation. Social habilitation signifies taking action to win opportunity for education, for decent standards of living, for a society that permits individuals to flourish. In short, it is called for whenever help is needed for victims of poverty, discrimination, grossly inadequate education, or a lack of vocational-professional opportunities. The term "social habilitation" may be somewhat less familiar than the term "social action." Both have the same meaning; both call for commitment and action.

Boehm unequivocally stated that such commitment and action require that social work underwrite (1) appropriate changes in the larger social structure, and (2) changes in the organizational and program pattern of social welfare resources. Furthermore, he said, social work should join with education and other professions in an attempt to reconstruct society when society chokes off the possibility of many men attaining their full physical, intellectual, esthetic, civic, and spiritual potential or when society holds itself to a low level of civilization.

130

This challenge evoked lively response in the conference discussions. The educator participants accepted the implicit offer of alliance between the professions of social work and education. Specifically, a school of education professor expressed the hope that social work would vigorously pursue a policy of social action rather than one of treating social pathology in terms of individual cases. He likened the individual case approach to employing band-aids to gushing arteries. Other educator participants indicated agreement by proposing some modification of "social foundations" courses offered prospective teachers so that students preparing for a degree in social work might jointly enroll in such courses with future teachers. They also suggested that school and community programs for ameliorating the lot of the poor or of families with multiple problems should be shared by education and social work. (Participants returned to a discussion of joint courses in a different context, as noted below.)

Persuasive evidence that an impressive number of leaders in education are prepared to work hand-in-hand with social work in improving the opportunities of children, youth, and adults who live in rural and urban slums was indicated in the papers of two educators and in the participants' response to them. Ole Sand in "The Teaching Profession" posed the question: "What is the school's role in dealing with serious national problems such as youth unemployment and juvenile delinquency?" [2] N. L. Gage in "Education of Teachers: Psychology of Education" discussed in particular education in the great cities.[3] He called for concerted action by education and social work in amelioration of social *malaise*. Discussion brought out the special obligation of the schools to improve the conditions of learning for the culturally disadvantaged and pointed up the opportunities the schools have to participate with social work in co-operative programs.

An area for potential collaboration between social work and education broader than that of bettering the chances of the culturally deprived was suggested by I. James Quillen in "Education of Teachers: Social Foundations." [4] Educator participants in supporting this suggestion stated that members of both professions should co-operate in efforts to make both the community and the school places where children of all backgrounds can develop and become effective individuals and citizens.

Social restoration. Turning to the second categorized objective of social work, social restoration, the conference considered the day-by-day activities of the social worker, and especially of the social worker

---

[2] *See* pp. 31–48.
[3] *See* pp. 86–103.
[4] *See* pp. 67–85.

in the school. The goal of social restoration, less ambitious than that of social habilitation, is to provide resources to sustain persons gravely handicapped in some way and to restore to normal social functioning persons who can be helped.

Discussion brought out that a mixture of success and failure was to be expected as a result of action taken by school teachers and administrators or by school social workers with students whose difficulties in school did not yield to help from the teacher. The point was frequently made that teachers and school social workers usually meet when the teacher experiences failure with a student. When Henry or Mary cannot seem to learn, when it is almost impossible to teach them, the school turns to its social worker, or its specialist in remedial reading, school psychologist, or other specialist for help.

FUNCTIONS OF THE SOCIAL WORKER IN THE SCHOOL

In discussing the functions of the social worker in the school, participants considered what happens when teacher and social worker confront one another. Will the school social worker be perceived by the teachers and principal of a school as an outside expert called in to rescue a teacher, or will he be perceived as a member of the school staff who is specially prepared both to keep the school informed about the community, neighborhood, or family background of all the students and to assist the school in communicating with other community agencies—police, courts, employment resources, and welfare services?

Institutional and residual models. Two alternative models of the social work role and function in the school were projected in exploring answers to this hypothetical question. When the social restoration objective of social work is analyzed within the setting of a school, it conventionally means helping a student attain a level of social functioning that will enable him to learn and make full use of his school experience. It is the lack of purposeful interaction between the student and the school, or his truancy, or delinquency that customarily brings the school social worker into the picture. The effectiveness of the school social worker's action may be conditioned by how he is perceived by one or more of the teachers, the principal, or others on the staff, and by how he perceives himself. Boehm identifies two perspectives or models—"residual" and "institutional":

> The institutional approach postulates that in modern society social institutions are interdependent because social needs and problems are interdependent. . . . The residual philosophy would invoke social work only after failure has occurred in attainment of their goals by such basic institutions as family, economy, church, and so on.

Discussion brought out that the institutional model is preferred by the social work profession and has competed successfully with the residual model. Some school social workers perform as though they were following the residual model, but their professional preparation has not endorsed this pattern. It was agreed that the desired view of the school social worker is that he is a helpful colleague of teachers, a useful member of the school team of specialists. Social work participants emphasized that school social workers should make clear to the school staff that they are colleagues professsionally prepared to offer special services complementing those of the classroom teacher and of other noninstructional specialists.

The social work profession traditionally has insisted that the school social worker think of himself as a member of the school's professional team, with the function of supplementing the central work of the school, namely instruction by teachers. Those responsible for the professional preparation of school social workers uniformly have insisted, although not always with success, that the school social worker is a specialist whose function is to collaborate with teachers by being useful to them in their work, which is at the heart of the school's function.

Turning from an attempt to assess these two models in terms of the school social worker's functioning per se, participants considered them in terms of effective communication between social workers and teachers.

In the residual model, communication between the teacher and all noninstructional personnel, including the social worker, is minimized by virtue of the teacher's superordinate position vis-à-vis subordinate specialists. No one of the subordinates is an equal of the teacher, who is the one person whose work—teaching—is the task for which the school is organized. It was noted that, according to this view, the individual student's learning and general development are ignored. When the teacher occupies the position implied by the residual model of school social work functioning it is illogical to expect him to communicate freely with subordinates.

In contrast, the institutional model seems to hold more promise for interprofessional communication. When the needs of a particular student require the special resources of the school social worker, he is brought into action. When the resources of some other noninstructional specialist are required, his services are made available. It was noted that this procedure puts primary emphasis on the teaching-learning task of the school.

Values, Objectives, and Functions of Formal Education

Discussion, taking as its point of departure the papers of Sand, Quillen, and Gage, noted above, disclosed that educators do not enjoy professional agreement on the values, objectives, and functions of education, comparable to the agreement found in the profession of social work. In general terms, there appears to be a continuum between two poles. At one pole are those who see the school as an agency charged by society to teach the three R's and the core of the knowledge that savants hold to be of most worth. It was observed that this end of the continuum may easily be broadened to include an obligation to teach the values on which a culture has consensus—provided there is such a consensus. At the other pole are those who hold that schools share social work's obligation to achieve social habilitation, which includes the social well-being of students and their acquisition of such skills as improve the likelihood of their being successful in pursuit of both instrumental and noninstrumental values.

The majority of the educator participants had need of both poles in spelling out their positions. A basic distinction in objectives for schools, provided by Sand, is between responsibilities that are almost exclusively those of the school and those that can be best met by joint efforts of the school and other social agencies. Participants did not address themselves to the implications of this distinction nor consider whether joint efforts of education and social work might be fruitful in the development of values and ideals, social and civic competence, and vocational preparation. Rather, they seemed to favor the residual perspective about social work. This may have been because in the strictly academic view of the school, all eyes are on the teacher and other members of the staff are thought to be employed only to help the teacher. In this view of education, the school social worker is one of the helpers; he is in the school to "cure" students who have become disciplinary problems or who have special difficulties in learning because of problems that stem from their environment outside school.

Some contrast with this attitude was provided by a view of education that expands the functions of the teacher. According to this view, the teacher's functions would include taking into account the social and emotional atmosphere of the classroom, the feelings of the students, and other factors that stem from the belief that the school supplements the home and other agencies and institutions in educating the young.

VALUES ESTEEMED BY THE SCHOOL

Discussion of values influencing American educational theory and practice disclosed that values of schoolmen (teachers and administrators) are similar to those of social workers. However, schoolmen and educators do not appear to be in agreement as to how these values are to be realized. The implication of this lack of agreement for the school social worker is that he has to learn the educational philosophy and policies of each school and school system in which he works.

Participants from the disciplines of both education and social work seemed to be in general agreement when the values of elementary and secondary education were stated at a high level of abstraction. For example, Sand's answer to the question, "What is good education?" was that which "enables the individual to function most effectively in his environment, to reach his own greatest potential, and to contribute constructively to the society in which he lives." This statement was never challenged in the give-and-take of the discussions and by inference it was accepted by the participants. Again, by inference, education and social work should encounter no difficulties in communicating about concepts of values. In effect, there is agreement that both social work and education are humane in orientation. Both are "helping professions," seeking to help men to realize themselves and to contribute to society.

OBJECTIVES AND FUNCTIONS OF EDUCATION

Conference discussion worked its way down from this acceptance of abstract values to consideration of how these values are implemented. As already noted, schoolmen hold diverse beliefs on the desirable functions of education, and it is recognized that controversy is to be expected when, in Sand's words, values act as "criteria for assessing present practices and as guides to future improvement of our schools. . . ."

There is a perennial dialogue among educators between "essentialists" and "progressives." The former hold that the learning of subject matter, values, and skills is the school's essential objective. The latter believe that a student will not learn to the extent of his capacity if he is perplexed by anxieties or handicapped in other ways by an unfortunate environment or by heredity. Thus the progressives hold that the student's development of sensibility, social conscience, compassion, warmth, and stability is of paramount importance. In this, they are closer than the essentialists to the philosophy that characterizes social work. Furthermore, while the essentialist believes that the school should perpetuate "the best" that civilization has achieved, the progressive joins with social workers in urging attention to social habilitation or at least social reconstruction aimed at creating a society in which poverty, war, and other threats to human dignity and achievement would be minimized.

This controversy divides educator from educator, rather than educator from social worker. However, the social worker, and specifically the school social worker, must be aware of these issues.

He needs to know what the schools consider must be done in the name of the values accepted by both professions.

Faced with the realities of this situation, the conference struggled with defining the objectives and functions of American education, taking as its point of departure the following formulation offered by Sand:

> The essential objectives of education, therefore, must be premised on a recognition that education is a process of changing behavior and that a changing society requires the capacity for self-teaching and self-adaptation. Priorities in educational objectives should be placed upon such goals as:
> 1. Learning how to learn, how to attack new problems, and how to acquire new knowledge.
> 2. Using rational processes.
> 3. Building competence in basic skills.
> 4. Developing intellectual and vocational competence.
> 5. Exploring values in new experience.
> 6. Understanding concepts and generalizations.

Above all, the school must develop in the pupil the ability to learn under his own initiative and an abiding interest in doing so.

It was recognized that these are specific objectives. Does their realization result in a teacher being less interested than a social worker in society, in social habilitation? In effect, general acceptance of these objectives by the conference challenged the educator participants to consider such issues as: Does the teacher's special concern or specialization mean that social restoration and social habilitation —purposes to which social workers are dedicated—must yield to preoccupation with subject matter, with methods of instruction and human learning?

It was not part of the assignment of the conference to spell out the curriculum of the schools, and discussion, accordingly, did not concern itself with this area. However, comparison of curricular blueprints would show how schools and school systems vary in interpreting some of the objective of education designated by Quillen: cultural transmission and socialization, richness in experience, identification with good models, and even such a seemingly straightforward objective as effective communication. The tensions between essentialists and progressives and between adherents of "operational values" developing from personal needs and of normative values regnant in the culture of a particular society—to use the distinction made by Sand—have produced conflicts among educators which call for difficult decisions. It is essential that social work be conscious of such decisions if there is to be effective communication between the two professions. Participants, in their discussions, did not arrive at the conclusion that educators had found a way out of their dilemma. There was, however, agreement among the educator participants that the schools should seek to make students aware of social problems and to develop in students the skills that are promising for attacking social problems. On the assumption that these participants represented educational leadership in the United States, this agreement may be said to signify acceptance by educators of Boehm's values of social restoration and social habilitation.

Comparison of Social Work and Education

It was agreed that there appear to be no significant differences in the values and long-range objectives of social work and education. In these areas the two professions converge, but each profession, as is to be expected, specializes in its functions. Specialization of effort in social work is different from specialization in education. Social work participants made clear that when the social worker enters the school, he is there to help the teacher. Stated in professional terms, the school social worker is a professional noninstructional member of whatever pupil-personnel service the school or school system provides.

SPECIAL CONCERN OF THE SCHOOL

Quillen pinpointed the special concern of the school in these words:

> All societies and cultures contain a variety of educative agencies. In American culture, these include the family, peer groups, the mass media, the church, child- and youth-serving agencies, and the community as a whole, as well as the school. The unique characteristic of the school is that it is established and maintained for the sole purpose of education.

Specialization of function is clearly delineated here. But, as Quillen acknowledged and participants pointed out, the schools need to co-operate with workers in other agencies who are seeking to meet educational needs. Because society is complex and subject to rapid change, co-operation and collaboration among specialists is mandatory.

Discussion sought to enumerate some of the issues that arise for teachers in the process of carrying out the specialized function of education. Should a teacher, whose objective is instruction, attend more to subject matter, instructional materials, and methods of teaching and learning than to the effects of the instruction on the quality of life that will be led by the student? Are the nature and problems of society as important to the teacher as subject matter, instructional materials, and methods of teaching and learning? Does realization of the specific objectives of education result in a teacher being less interested than a social worker in mankind, in society, in social habilitation? Does the teacher's special concern or specialization of function mean that social restoration and social habilitation —purposes to which social workers are dedicated—must yield to preoccupation with subject matter, methods of instruction, and human learning?

No ready answers were found—or even sought—for these questions.

SPECIAL CONCERN OF SOCIAL WORK

By inference, social work participants appeared to provide some answers by expressing the hope that education would join with social work in urging social action or social habilitation needed for an effective attack on social problems. In doing so, these participants recognized the widespread belief among educators that the schools intend to help with social habilitation, especially in urban programs, and they welcomed this intention.

A parallel concern among educators in the area of social restoration was not discernible. Put another way, discussion brought out that social work's special concern for social habilitation—embracing among other actions warring on poverty, winning equality of opportunity in all spheres and for all minorities—was shared by education. There appeared, however, to be no similar unity of social work and education in the area of social restoration. The restoration of adequate social functioning, work with multiproblem families, securing help for youth and for families from a variety of helping agencies in the community—all this appeared to be the concern of social work but not of the schools.

IMPLICATIONS FOR INTERPROFESSIONAL COMMUNICATION

The similarities and differences in values, objectives, and functions of social work and education were recognized by the participants as having direct implications for interprofessional communication. To sum up: it was agreed that the two professions hold congruent values at a high level of abstraction. Below this level, however, the values, objectives, and functions of social work are more clearly defined and more generally accepted by the profession than is the case for the values, objectives, and functions of education. This situation gives rise to difficulties in interprofessional communication that must be faced if progress is to be made. Two specific difficulties were noted and served as a springboard for extended discussion of the problems of communication and their possible solution.

As already stated, there is a lack of consensus within the profession of education on specific objectives and functions, despite the fact that there is agreement on values if they are abstract and not spelled out in terms of day-by-day activities. Because of this lack, social workers cannot be certain on what basis a specific school or school system actually operates in respect to the values, objectives, and functions presumably espoused by the profession of education as a whole.

A second difficulty centers on how the social worker's role is perceived in the school or school system. Social work holds that the functions of social workers in the schools can be spelled out as distinct from the schools' primary function; nevertheless, the social work function is both complementary and supplementary to the school's function. This seeming contradiction creates difficulty or, at the least, confusion.

The teacher's essential task, it is generally agreed, is to educate all students in a common curriculum; the school social worker's essential task is to assist the school by restoring to full functioning those students who for a variety of reasons are handicapped in learning effectively. Both the residual and institutional models, described and discussed above, fit this social work role. The consensus of the conference was overwhelmingly in favor of the institutional model. Whichever model obtains in a school or a school system, the social worker is not perceived and used in a uniform and predictable way; he is used differently by different principals and teachers. Herein lies a roadblock in achieving interprofessional communication.

Opportunities for Co-operation Through Professional Preparation

Discussion of the difficulties in communication noted above uncovered the need for clarification of the respective roles of teacher and social worker and for clearer perception by members of each profession of the role of the other profession. Suggestions for achieving these ends were offered and discussed.

Several participants proposed that university schools of social work and schools or departments of education should explore the possibilities for common experiences in the preparation of both teachers and social workers. Discussion of this proposal led the conference into consideration of educational foundations common to both professions, and of how to include them in the professional preparation of teachers and social workers.

It was readily agreed that urbanization is one of the chief reasons for improving communication between social work and education. Urbanization and alterations in patterns of work, induced by changes in science and technology, explain "the characteristic pathology of the urban proletariat," as one participant put it. They explain "its alienation from, and sometimes hostility to, middle-class values and aspirations, its economic insecurity, heightened by automation, and its despair." Education, equally with social work, confronts these conditions of modern urban life and the meaning of these conditions for students, especially those from the lower socioeconomic group.

Both professions also confront other conditions that have a direct bearing on the problems of children and youth. The following were noted in the discussions: 30 percent of mothers who work have children under 18 years of age, and half of these mothers have children under the age of 6. About 11 percent of children and youth under 18 come from homes broken by death, divorce, or desertion. The physical mobility of American families may increase the insecurity of children, even when the move is advantageous for the family. Almost 12 million young people move from one house to another every year; and of these, 2 million move from one state to another.[5]

Despite the fact that community and social conditions impinge on both professions, it was acknowledged that preparation in these areas is utilized differently by social workers and by teachers and school administrators. Since the teacher's role is played in the school, the student teacher receives his training almost exclusively in the school, and not in work with out-of-school youth groups. In contrast, the student in social work may have his field instruction in schools, but he may also work in welfare agencies, hospitals, and a variety of other community settings.

Students in schools of social work study human behavior and social environment, and also, not infrequently, other social sciences. Through such study the student learns about social disorganization and how to deal with the problems of social habilitation and social restoration with which social work historically copes. There is a paucity of comparable sources for student teachers.

In considering the feasibility of courses for students in both professions covering material for which they have common need, the following points were made:

1. Both teachers and social workers need knowledge about human growth and development, theories of human learning, family organization, community resources, and related types of information.

2. The application of this knowledge differs for teachers, social workers and, for that matter, for nurses, psychologists, and members of other professions.

3. A practical problem arises because professional training for

---

[5] Hyrum M. Smith, "Pupil Personnel Services," in Horace W. Lundberg, ed., *School Social Work* (Washington, D.C.: U.S. Department of Health, Education and Welfare, Bulletin No. 15, 1964), p. 20.

teaching is usually at the undergraduate level, while that for social work is at the postgraduate level.

4. Taking the above points into consideration the most feasible plan might be for undergraduate pre-professional study to include basic courses in psychology and the social sciences, perhaps taken jointly, and for graduate programs in the respective disciplines to emphasize applied knowledge, that is, its utilization.

5. The graduate professional program of each profession would have its own distinctive character, but opportunities would be sought for common interprofessional experience. A prime area for such interprofessional study, it was suggested, is study of the school as a social institution. Since compulsory education makes experience with public or private schools well-nigh universal, a course on the school as a social institution would be widely useful.

There was general agreement on the desirability of exploring the usefulness and feasibility of such a course offered on an interprofessional basis, with the stricture that the realities of local campus conditions should be taken into account.

SOCIAL AND PSYCHOLOGICAL FOUNDATION COURSES

It was repeatedly pointed out by social work participants that social work is an applied field. Hence, its practitioners must know the facts as well as the theory of social classes, intergroup relations, social mobility, and other topics conventionally embraced by sociology. Typically, the social work student, in his preparation for the degree of master of social work, augments study of human behavior and social environment with detailed attention to social welfare policy, to communities, their social pathology, and the resources that are available and might be available for social habilitation and restoration. Thus the study of social theory and action is one of the bases on which social work builds its professional curriculum. In this curriculum, the study of, and training in, community settings augment the social foundation courses.

Turning to the preparation of teachers, discussion brought out an important difference between the preparation of teachers through courses usually termed "social foundations of education" and the preparation of social workers, summarized above. This difference is that student social workers are trained to apply what they learn about communities and community resources or lack of resources, while student teachers conventionally are not given comparable experience in applying what they learn in courses on the social foundations of education.

Social work participants repeatedly referred to the efforts of the

141

social work profession to obtain from city, state, and federal govern-
ments improved opportunities for the poor, more adequate programs of assistance, such as Aid to Dependent Children, and other
action for the betterment of society. The humanitarianism of social
work was emphasized again and again throughout the discussions.
Educator participants, on the one hand, approved of humanitarianism as a value that teachers should hold; on the other hand, they
indicated that education's responsibility for teaching was so great
that it was impractical to siphon off a considerable amount of effort
into social action.

Gage countered this second view in his paper.[6] He expressed
clearly and vigorously the belief that educators have an obligation
to use their skills for children, youth, and adults in our society who
are the victims of poverty, subject to the alienation of life in a large
city, unemployed because of automation, lack of education, or other
reasons. Fully one-third of Gage's paper was devoted to "educational
psychology in the great cities" and described research in educational
psychology that has recently been published or that can be undertaken. Thus, participants saw that even the educational psychologists, the most research-bent of all educators, are concerned with
what can be done to free and to strengthen the intellectual abilities,
achievement, attitudes, interests, and emotional, physical, and social
adjustment of urban children and youth.

Participants—both educators and social workers—concluded that
the joint concern of both professions with humanitarianism provides a basis for collaborative efforts. At present, however, preparation for social work is more social-action directed than preparation
for teaching.

In pursuing this idea, discussion turned to the social conscience
manifested by present patterns of teacher preparation. One participant, dean of a school of education, made the point that when the
objectives of education are under scrutiny there are confusions
about such concepts as equality, civil liberties, democratic process
in decision-making, the nature of social and cultural progress.
Teachers, he said, ought to think about the values involved in such
issues, read about them, and discuss them. Such efforts might well
precede any social action on the part of educators, but this timing
does not imply that the teacher should abandon or even postpone
his idealistic viewpoint.

There appeared to be agreement that the teacher should collaborate with social workers and others in social action or habilitation
—the latter term was used throughout the discussions—but that his
role is chiefly to teach students how to think, how to communicate,

---

[6] *See* pp. 97–103.

how to give serious thought to social problems, how to work with others in the assault on social problems rather than to take action for specific social ends. Transferring this general concept into the school setting, the instructional specialist—that is, the teacher, principal, and school administrators are partners in social action with noninstructional specialists; indeed, they are perhaps the less active partners.

Within this frame of reference, discussion turned to the courses on the social foundations of education which are typically part of the curriculum of teacher preparation, and the possibility of using such courses for joint study by student teachers and student social workers. Social foundation courses are undergoing a transformation that is significant for such joint experience and for interprofessional communication. Quillen in his paper noted that two seemingly conflicting trends are responsible for this transformation: "The broadening of the conception of the field of education and the emergence of a sharper focus and a more concerted emphasis on the field within the discipline of sociology under the name of the sociology of education." The former denotes serious attention, at long last, to the process of education by political scientists, economists, social psychologists, and anthropologists. Within the discipline of sociology, educational sociology has been a weak field in comparison with other areas of applied sociology, such as the sociology of medicine, nursing, or criminology.

EDUCATIONAL SOCIOLOGY

Participants also considered possible opportunities for communication and collaboration between education and social work in the area of educational sociology. Among the many topics embraced by educational sociology, they pinpointed those in which social work as well as education has such obvious interest that joint courses at a graduate level might be designed for both professions.

Specific suggestions were made as follows: On as many campuses as possible, representatives of both schools of social work and schools of education should review the possibility of joint instruction. Joint graduate seminars were considered specially promising. These seminars would utilize the sociologist's and the social psychologist's interest in the school and classroom as social systems. The role and function of each specialist would be reviewed and from such study students in each profession would learn about the objectives and responsibilities of the other profession. Two questions were proposed to indicate the typical content of such seminars: What do social workers wish to know about teaching and the school? What do teachers wish to know about social work and community resources?

PSYCHOLOGY COMMON TO BOTH PROFESSIONS

There was general agreement that materials drawn from all the social sciences could contribute to a graduate seminar or course on contemporary social thought pertinent to the professions, and that such a seminar or course might be open to persons preparing to be either social workers or schoolmen. As with the suggestion for joint courses or seminars for student social workers and student teachers, discussed above, it was recognized that the first step would have to be discussion by leaders of both professions on individual campuses. The next step might be a conference of representatives of the two disciplines.

Although no attempt was made to spell out content of these suggested courses, discussion noted the overlap in the psychology that is studied by social workers-in-training and teachers-in-training. Gage in his paper noted the growing attention in educational literature to problems of learning, of motivation, and of measuring intelligence among underprivileged pupils, especially those in the slums of large cities. This indication of social awareness in education is a new trend; it is noteworthy and directly relevant to the problem of interprofessional communication. Social work participants reported a change in the psychology taught to social worker students, which is also relevant to the conference topic. Traditionally in social work education psychoanalytic psychology has been mined to provide both a theoretical framework and practical clues for understanding the feelings, attitudes, and behavior of clients. This approach is now being broadened to include learning theory and the study of growth and development.

Educational psychology and the psychology taught to student social workers are drawing closer together. The incisive explanation, on which the participants agreed, is that social work students are learning more about normal behavior and students in education are learning more about abnormal behavior. Both groups start with the common assumption that human behavior is not arbitrary and irrational, but can be explained; both are becoming accustomed to considering competing and complementary explanations about what causes behavior. As one participant put it, educational psychology is no longer dominated by Thorndike and social work psychology is no longer dominated by Freud, or by Jung, Adler, or some other analytic psychologist.

Despite recognition that content of joint courses in social psychology should be worked out by representatives of the two disciplines at individual campuses, the idea was so attractive to the participants that they identified specific areas in which social workers and teachers could learn from one another's research. Group work in social work and the learning theory in education were singled out as examples. One participant, a professor of social work, said that she found work done by psychologists on identification and learning theory specially useful for social workers. Educator participants, in turn, noted the potential value of group work in the preparation of teachers. Social workers learn the process of working with groups; teachers, it was said, have similar need to learn the group process. Some participants pointed out that psychology is becoming a part of the core subject, educational psychology. On balance, however, educator participants held that the psychology of education is given less weight in teacher training than the areas of learning, growth, and development, emotional and social adjustment, and educational measurements and evaluation.

In the discussion of tests, measures, and scientific assessment, social work participants expressed the hope that social work education would increasingly take more note of empirical evaluation, which characterizes education. They pointed out, however, that educators sometimes put more trust in measures of intelligence and other measures of ability than social workers feel the measuring instruments justify. In essence, social work is optimistic about what individuals can be and do, if only their environment is favorable. There is no comparable optimism among educators. Some are inclined to be environmentalists; others feel that when relatively culture-free tests of intelligence and special abilities are developed they will show generally unmodifiable differences among individuals in their abilities to learn, in their motivation, and their ideals.

These considerations were indicative of differences of approach in the two disciplines which must be taken into account in developing the joint courses proposed by the conference.

A unifying element, which to some extent compensates for differences in approach, is the trend toward research habits and attitudes manifest in the educational programs of both social work and education. This trend toward emphasis on research may be expected to provide a bridge between the two professions and to further interprofessional communication.

Learning About Another Professional Role

The discussions on the social and psychological foundations of social work and education and on possible modifications in professional preparation, summarized above, were characterized by general agreement and general acceptance of suggestions offered. By contrast, discussion of how the social worker and the teacher can understand each other's role gave rise to sharp differences of opinion.

Taking a course together, it was said, is an intellectual pursuit and a necessary one but it is not the only road to effective communication; it does not automatically make it possible for the two professions to work together. To achieve this goal, teacher and social worker must learn each other's professional role.

Some participants suggested that the student social worker, with the planning and help of an experienced teacher, might take the role of teacher for a few days in order to gain an understanding of that role; in similar fashion, the student teacher, with the planning and help of an experienced school social worker, might take the role of a social worker, at least to the extent of making a few home visits.

There were reactions against this suggestion from participants who were faculty members of schools of education and schools of social work. An attempt to understand another person's professional role through role assumption was held to be impractical and, more important, untenable, since it would be a denial of the necessity for professional training. Teacher and social worker, however, can understand each other's role by learning about each profession's role expectations. This, it was emphasized, is quite a different matter from role assumption. Various ways of clarifying role expectations were suggested: the teacher and the social worker in their professional interaction should each clearly define his own role; each should observe how the other one fills his role, with opportunity for questions and discussion; and there might be joint study of practice for student teachers and student social workers.

AREAS OF POSSIBLE FRICTION

An attempt was made to identify some of the areas of conflict and to suggest constructive solutions.

According to the usual pattern in a school, students having difficulty are referred to the school social worker and other noninstructional personnel. Complicated reactions accompany this seemingly simple and clear-cut procedure. The teacher may well dislike the student who has been responsible for what he considers his failure in his own profession, and he may resent the school social worker for a number of reasons. One is that the social worker may seem to the teacher to be overly sympathetic to the student. Another is that the very presence of a social worker on the staff may signify to the teacher: "There is a person who thinks that he can handle a student whom I could not help, no matter what I did." And—human nature being what it is—the social worker's success may well increase the teacher's resentment.

Another difficulty is that often the school social worker has not learned enough about schools to feel at home in them—to understand the professional jargon, the main focus and objectives of the instructional staff, and the adminstrative set-up. Administrative direction and acceptance of the school social worker is sometimes unclear or entirely lacking. Under these circumstances, teachers are uncertain about whether, or the extent to which, they should use the services of the school social worker, and social workers are sometimes tempted to bypass the administrative structure and confer with teachers at a somewhat unofficial level, which is often unsatisfactory to all concerned.

A more subtle difficulty stems from the fact that when the social worker enters the picture, he shares the child with the teacher, and with the parents, too. His expectations for the child may be quite different from the teacher's, and from the expectations of the parents and the child himself. All these factors create tensions and hamper interprofessional communication.

A major source of strain is the difference in role perception of educators and school social workers and their different orientations. The school social worker, it was noted, relates professionally with social workers employed elsewhere in the community, and these professional ties modify his role within the school to a greater extent than do the professional ties of the teacher. The school social worker also differs from the teacher in that he is actively connected with the community-wide social work system and at the same time he is part of a specific school system. The teacher, obviously, does not have comparable affiliations with two distinct systems.

The school social worker, by the very nature of his profession and his role in the school, is involved in the community. He is often the school's agent for intimate contact with parents of students with special problems; he must know a good deal about the family, home-life, and neighborhood of each student referred to him; he must know about family and children's services and other community resources, in order to effect appropriate referral, either himself, or through the school principal or other official.

Participants focused on this away-from-school professional life of the school social worker because it hints at problems in communication with teachers and other school personnel who are less community-oriented and more school-bound in their daily work. The fact that the school social worker spends a good deal of his time outside the school, as he must in carrying out his professional assignment, may signal to other staff members, and especially to teachers, that his goals are not the same as theirs, despite the fact that he has been assigned to the school. When the school social worker's role is thus perceived as essentially nonacademic, communication problems are likely to be present.

The Conference

The principal's position in the hierarchical structure of the school has been noted above. The social worker encounters difficulties if the principal's role is not clearly perceived by himself and by the school staff, and these difficulties are compounded by the fact that the administrative habits of principals are not uniform.

Some principals use the school social worker chiefly to enlist the assistance of psychiatrists or social workers attached to clinics or social agencies. Some find the school social worker the most useful liaison with the juvenile courts, probation officers, or the police. Still others consult with the school social worker on the assumption that he is the best-informed person on the staff in the psychodynamics of student behavior. In short, the principal is the person in the school system who defines the status of the school social worker and determines how he is used in a specific school.

In the context of how to achieve better understanding of role expectations of another professional, the principal's role and the effect of how his role is perceived by the school's instructional and noninstructional staff members were explored. Participants were in agreement that ideally the principal exercises leadership within the school. He is the key person in recognizing friction between staff members and stands ready to give help, when needed, in achieving co-operative relationships. It was noted that the Interprofessional Research Commission on Pupil Personnel Services has considered the role and function of the school principal as a subject for high-priority research—an indication of the importance of the principal's role. Participants returned to a discussion of the principal's role when they considered specific action for improving interprofessional communication within the schools.

It was proposed that the principal's leadership role and his sensitivity to the professional roles of specialists within the school be highlighted in the professional preparation of principals, and that departments of education, schools of social work, and school systems consider the idea of interprofessional seminars and workshops in which the points of friction between professional personnel in the schools can be discussed and resolved.

Theories of Interprofessional Communication

Day-by-day interprofessional communication in the schools is among social workers, teachers, principals, guidance counselors, school psychologists, school nurses, and other noninstructional specialists. Each of the schools within which these professional persons function may be considered by a student of communication as a closed system. The term means a system in which the staff is hierarchically organized with more or less clearly defined and assigned functions. In a school, the principal typically assigns staff functions, and the instructional and noninstructional staff members relate and communicate, with varying degrees of success, within the hierarchical organization of the system. By virtue of being a system, the school in its operation lends itself to study by sociologists, social psychologists, or students of communication. The conference, of course, was not concerned with systems-analysis in depth, but with analysis of communication as it affects the relationships of educators and school social workers. Within this frame of reference, participants surveyed the theoretical schemes for communication analysis presented in Erasmus L. Hoch's paper and their application to interprofessional communication between social work and education.[7]

GAME THEORY

It was perhaps indicative of the co-operative spirit and high hopes for interprofessional communication motivating the conference that participants appeared to be unwilling to identify the relationship of education and social work with game theory. Hoch explains that game theory is a "theoretical attempt to throw some light on just what is involved when groups and their representatives try to find their place in a hierarchy vis-à-vis each other." To the discussants, this theory spelled rivalry, a form of competition in which only one player can win. In effect they rejected the possibility that the two professions might be rivals at some time or with respect to some subgroup, such as school guidance counselors.

Only one conclusion was drawn from the discussion. Gaming may be inevitable, the thought ran, but at least for the near future it is inconceivable that education and social work would sacrifice collaboration for rivalry, since the two professions face enormous social problems that call for the combined use of each profession's special competence.

BEHAVIOR SYSTEMS THEORY

Analysis of behavior systems calls for inventories of "inputs," such as information, and "outputs," that is, responses of one sort or another. Unfortunately, from the point of view of successful communication, it is difficult to predict the responses to inputs in social work–education relationships. The most vexing input problem in communication between social workers and teachers—and between any distinct professional groups—is terminology. A participant who is a professor of social work illustrated this point by

---

[7] *See* "Theories of Interprofessional Communication," pp. 104–125.

the term "identification" which has different connotations for educators, social workers, educational psychologists, and so on. She said:

> I have found that "identification" as used by the teacher has to do with cognitive or intellectual attachment, continuing manner and behavior of the teacher, producing a change in perception. As used by the social worker, identification connotes catharsis, a feeling about, an attachment for, acceptance of and acceptance by. This may be one of those terms that we use together but use differently.

Another participant, also a professor of social work, pointed out blocks to communication between teachers and social workers, each associated with what they regard as a student's progress. Terminology was at the root of the difficulty. She put it this way:

> There are subsidiary values attached to the technical processes of teaching and of social work which differ from each other and may even be incompatible with each other. For example, most social workers attach a high value to a child's ability to express and discuss negative feelings. This comes from our professional assumptions that such feelings, if unexpressed, have much to do with both delinquent and neurotic behavior. We see a child's ability to express anger and hostility as a reflection of our skill in helping him. Most teachers do not place a high value on this ability. It may be threatening to the teacher if the child expresses strong, angry feelings. Since a teacher must have a good degree of order in the class in order to carry on the skilled teaching of content, it is only natural that he places a high value on the child's ability to cooperate.

Several proposals were made for removing the roadblocks of terminology. University programs for training social workers and for training teachers should utilize opportunities for instructing these students in the technical vocabularies of the two professions and, more important, in the professions' objectives and values. For example, aggression and acting out by a student is viewed by the social worker as symptomatic and even desirable in some instances, but it is usually viewed as disruptive and threatening by the teacher.

The teachers and social workers who are aware of the differing views of the two professions are less likely to irritate each other. For this reason, student teachers and student social workers need to recognize that these different views reflect differences in short-run professional goals. The short-run goal of the teacher is to promote learning; that of the school social worker is to help the student to function more adequately in his role as a pupil. The long-run goals of both teacher and school social worker converge, since the ultimate goal of both professions is to help students to become fully functioning human beings.

Each profession would profit from some knowledge of the other profession's premises about personality and behavior. Discussion of contrasting and even antagonistic beliefs in seminars or workshops attended by social work students and student teachers, or even by full-fledged professionals, was proposed. At the very least, each group would realize that the other one is acting on the basis of rational theories. A more far-reaching result might be research on human learning and personality development that would attempt to determine approaches to the aggressive students that hold greater promise for their academic rehabilitation.

COMMUNICATION AND INFORMATION THEORY

Hoch's paper underlined the frequency with which bias thwarts communication between two professions. Information exchanged by social workers and teachers is quite easily distorted because, in Hoch's words, it is "abbreviated, condensed, appreciably less detailed" than it should be for ready understanding and "arbitrarily categorized." It can be distorted to please the receiver or be heard in terms that the receiver expects to hear. Participants made no specific response to Hoch's observations about bias except to note that undergraduate education might make a contribution here by fostering effective listening as well as effective written and spoken communication.

MODELS OF ATTITUDE CHANGE

Referring to "the gulf of mutual incomprehension," which C. P. Snow says parts the two cultures, science and humanities, Hoch warned that social workers and educators should make certain that they do not "have a curiously distorted image of each other." Discussion of this point focused on the warped images of social work and teaching that are so often present in the school. Several participants urged that these images, which largely determine the attitude of one professional group toward another, be attacked through accurate information.

RESEARCH

The discussion of the four theoretical approaches, summarized above, carried implications for needed research. It would be helpful to know just where the paths of social workers and educators cross, what problems and circumstances usually bring the two professions together. Another area for research is the status-rating educators accord to social workers, and social workers accord to educators. Does one group feel threatened by the other? Does one see the other as having commanding power, responsibility, or authority? Improved interprofessional communication rests on the gathering of such facts. At the same time, there is need, in Hoch's words, "of some master taxonomers who can lay out the data on a conceptual matrix that will yield the theoretical understanding of professional relations in a way that immersion in day-by-day problems cannot."

Improvement in Interprofessional Communication

To some extent summing up discussions of the various aspects of interprofessional communication, participants considered how communication might be improved within the schools, within the community, and within the university—the locus of professional preparation.

IMPROVEMENT WITHIN THE SCHOOLS

The values held by persons who are seeking to improve communication with one another have force, it was pointed out; because values are the determinants of attitudes, biases, viewpoints, and even of the manner in which signals or meanings are interpreted. In this context, discussion returned to a consideration of the residual and institutional models of the role of the social worker in the school. The far-reaching effects of these models on communication between teacher and social worker were recognized.

Ideally, it was said, every school system should have social workers on its staff, and every school system should understand the functions of the school social worker. The current situation, however, does not begin to approach this ideal. Most school systems in the United States do not employ social workers, and in some communities that do employ school social workers each worker serves several schools, spending from one-half to one day a week in each. The gap between theory and practice is in part attributable to the fact that many school systems are not yet ready to accept the potential contributions of the school social worker, and in part to manpower shortages of social workers. These conditions must be taken into account in considering interprofessional communication in the school.

Another relevant factor is that individual schools differ in various ways. They differ in their educational philosophy; they may differ in policies of discipline or acceptable classroom behavior of students, and procedures about report cards, promotions, probation, parent-teacher conferences, and so on; they may differ on such seemingly trivial matters as how incoming messages, telephone calls, and mail are handled, how the faculty room is used, and the influence of school secretaries. All these factors, taken together, have a bearing on how successfully the school social worker relates with other members of the school staff.

The main-line job. Borrowing a term used by sociologists in the study of organizations, participants stressed that the "main-line job" of the school is teaching. The instructional staff readily identifies with this job, but the noninstructional staff can identify with it only obliquely. In discussing the implications of this situation, participants noted that the school social worker, as a professional specialist, faces the problems that beset all specialists who are not directly concerned with the main-line job of the organization in which they are working. The school social worker has a tendency to focus on his own specialty; he is likely to identify with his social work colleagues, whose values and objectives he shares. This professional identification is sometimes so strong that it weakens his ties with teachers, despite the fact that these are crucial for effective communication.

Basic tasks of the school social worker. Emphasizing that teachers and principals must understand what the school social worker does, if there is to be interprofessional communication, participants summarized the social worker's tasks as follows: (1) casework service to students and/or parents, (2) group work service for selected students, (3) collaboration with other school personnel, and (4) consultation with teachers, principals, and others in behalf of students in need of restorative help. Each of these tasks is carried on in the frame of reference of social work's objective of enhancing social functioning. In the school setting, this objective means enhancing the school performance of students whose performance is definitely unsatisfactory. It was noted that in the elementary school unsatisfactory behavior is generally academic failure or attention-getting and/or aggressive action; in the secondary school absenteeism becomes the chief problem.

Basic tasks of the principal. Recapitulating earlier discussion of the principal as the key person in the school organization, participants noted that he can nurture interprofessional communication in many ways. Two were singled out, as a matter of emphasis. The principal can hold carefully planned conferences for the entire staff—instructional and noninstructional—focusing on student and school problems that demand interprofessional action. He can also define how the service of the school social worker (and other noninstructional personnel) will be used and make clear their relation to the central objectives of the school.

Pursuing the idea of the strategic position of the principal in interprofessional communication, specific suggestions about his work were offered. He should be a leader. He should not assume that noninstructional specialists in student personnel services will automatically become "members of the team," but should take responsibility for the integration of these specialists with the instructional staff. He should provide in-service training in communication and collaboration for all of the staff, in which insights into the behavior of teachers, social workers, and other staff members are frankly discussed, and values and objectives held in common are recognized.

One further suggestion was made, having to do with mechanics, but nevertheless considered of far-reaching importance. The principal should provide for the social worker the facilities he needs in carrying on his work: a private office or some other arrangement that insures privacy for consultation with clients, locked files, a telephone, mail and message service, and secretarial help. The principal should make clear to the staff that these facilities are not granted as a special favor, but are necessary tools.

Individuals and groups. Reference was repeatedly made in the discussions to one impediment to effective communication between teachers and school social workers, namely, that teachers deal with groups of students and social workers deal with individual students.

In seeking how to cope with this apparent difficulty, the following observations were made. Teachers learn about individual differences in growth, development, reading readiness, rates of learning, and so on in their professional preparation. Nevertheless, they have to instruct groups, which range from 30 or 40 children in the elementary grades to an aggregate of possibly 150 students in the classes they instruct in junior and senior high school. Social workers learn how to work with individual students, but also learn group process, and some of them are learning how to counsel in groups. It was concluded that both teachers and social workers need to learn more about group process, communication systems within groups, leadership, and other topics that are the concern of social psychology. When they are more at home in this general area, the cleavage that is now sensed between those who work with groups and those who work with individuals will disappear, or at least seem less marked.

Generalizing from these observations, participants agreed that more knowledge about working with both individuals and groups would benefit teachers and school social workers in carrying out their assigned functions and also in promoting mutual understanding. At present, most social workers in schools have more experience with individuals, teachers have more experience with groups. The social worker should realize that he has been conditioned by his education to support his clients—in the school, the clients are the students referred to him—and that this conditioning may make him react antagonistically to the teacher and/or the principal. The teacher should try to free himself from irritation and even anger toward disturbing students; he may then be able to think about the causes of their behavior and possible therapeutic help. Participants realized that the objectivity implied in these suggestions is difficult for all concerned, but the rewards in terms of improved interprofessional communication are great.

IMPROVEMENT WITHIN THE COMMUNITY

Turning from the school to the community, in which opportunities for interprofessional communication are both great and unexplored, discussion touched on new educational forms, as embodied in the concept of the community school. The school of the future may place less emphasis on conventional academic skills and subject matter and more on the life, problems, and opportunities of the community. Participants vigorously expressed the view that schools as they now exist have not been used with optimum effectiveness and that until they are, it is premature to speculate on new educational forms. As one participant put it, "if there are too few school social workers, if co-ordination of schools with community agencies is inadequate, these lacks should be repaired. Then, if the schools were still inadequate, trial of new forms would be warranted." Other participants, however, held that it was useful and constructive to consider the trend toward the community school and the co-ordinated community welfare center and at the very least to envisage what the future may hold.

Following this line of thought, there was enough speculation about the community school to invite further study. Better interpersonal communication was implied, since the school social worker would be perceived as the staff member best equipped to co-ordinate family, neighborhood, and community resources. In exploring this idea, a note of caution was sounded. Briefly, the point was made that all resources cannot be offered or used in a single pattern. The neighborhood should not be oversold, since families are mobile, and the metropolitan or regional development of resources may often be more effective than the more restricted ones of a community.

The co-ordinated welfare center, as it is now being developed, may at some future time involve schools and school systems. Participants who suggested this development used the phrase "family of professions" to indicate the hope of effective and co-ordinated work by the "helping professions," which include social work and, to some extent, education. It was not suggested that it would be desirable for each profession to submerge its identity; rather, that there would be true interprofessional communication and co-ordination of efforts.

IMPROVEMENT WITHIN THE UNIVERSITY

In exploring how the training period for teachers and social workers might be used to give each profession a better understanding of the other one, participants first addressed themselves to the categorical question, what should future social workers learn about schools? A professor of social work urged that social work students and graduate social workers, too, should guard against projecting their own memories of school onto the school of today. The stereotype of punishment, rote learning, pointless and irrelevant materials, and poorly equipped schools is apt to be false. Present-day teachers usually have values and attitudes toward students that closely parallel social workers' values and their attitudes toward clients. Both seek the emancipation of individuals from the oppression of ignorance and stultifying environment; both seek to develop fully functioning human beings.

Thus the future social worker must learn what schools are actually like, what teachers and administrators are trying to do, and why they sometimes appear to have a different attitude toward students than the social worker has. As indicated frequently in the conference discussion of other facets of communication, much of the conflict between the school social worker and the teacher is rooted in their differing ways of perceiving and reacting to the disturbing student. If the social worker, in the course of his training, gains a better understanding of the values, objectives, and functions of education and a greater awareness of the teacher's day-by-day activities and problems, this conflict has a good chance of being resolved.

Turning to the companion question, what should future teachers and school administrators learn about social work, participants noted that teachers-in-training rarely learn anything about social work. As a result, they have false stereotypes about what social workers do and misleading expectations about social work—its values, objectives, and functions.

A participant who is a professor of social work offered a suggestion for counteracting this difficulty. Social work has knowledge of family, neighborhood, and community influences that would be valuable as curriculum material for courses in teacher education. Moreover, teacher education might well take a cue from social work education, which teaches empathy with a client and objectivity to the client's values and problems as perceived by the client. There is little comparable effort in supervised student teaching and in the methods courses that are a part of teacher education to develop the ability to understand another person's feelings and ideas. The process of teaching, rather than the process of student learning is emphasized and student teachers seldom learn how much the perceptions and feelings of students condition what they learn. The point was made that if student teachers were given such educational opportunities and also learned to be self-critical, they might be less prone to feeling defensive when students are troublesome.

The results of such a change of attitude in terms of relations with school social workers are obvious and were repeatedly noted in the discussion.

A final suggestion for improving interprofessional communication within the university was that classes in measurement and statistics in colleges and departments of education be opened to students in schools of social work. The suggestion was favored, in part because resources in the academic world are always relatively scarce and such a move would be a way of utilizing them more fully. The chief advantage was seen as a strengthening of interprofessional communication. Many psychologists, it was pointed out, have similar arrangements with schools of education. Social work is becoming increasingly interested in tests and measurements and with experimental assessment of various kinds of treatment; education is even more involved with tests, measurements, and experimentation. Thus, the subject matter is sufficiently common to both education and social work for the social work student to benefit from the experience.

Call to Action

Both education and social work assume that men are educable, that behavior can be altered, although not miraculously. Both disciplines, it was noted throughout the discussion, have common values and objectives. As was clearly brought out in the conference papers and discussion taken as a whole, both are aware of the need for building a better world, and both in their different ways, indicated by the nature of their functions, can stand together in pressing for more adequate treatment of conditions that can be remedied.

part III

THE CHALLENGE

8

THE CHALLENGE TO THE
TWO PROFESSIONS

By Samuel H. Popper

The theme of the Conference on Interprofessional Communication has been called a communication challenge. Formidable as this challenge might seem at close range, four days of discussion have made it clear that the challenge of interprofessional communication between education and social work is but one aspect of a much more formidable challenge that now confronts the American social system. This response, therefore, has three objectives:

1. To suggest a conceptualization of the more formidable challenge and to use it as a framework in which to set the principal ideas that have been delineated in the papers and in the discussions of this conference.

2. To highlight those areas in the professional structures of education and social work that have been identified by the conference as sources of the imperatives for planned interprofessional communication.

3. To explore with some specificity the important question of future direction.

Background of the Challenge

The substantive meaning of this conference expresses a determination in the professional sectors of education and social work to conserve the institutionalized value system of our society in an age of slums, suburbs, and the cybernetic revolution. Future generations will take the record of this conference as evidence of its steadfast belief that the democratic and humanistic values of American society constitute a most precious asset. Some of these values have been stated eloquently in the papers prepared for the conference by Smalley, Boehm, and Sand. Smalley's paper reviewed a tradition

161

in professional social work that is concerned with "people as whole human beings, in relationship to other people and within the context, structures, and institutional forms of a society." The goal of releasing human power for the attainment of social progress, it is important to note, is shared by both education and social work.

The alliance of the two professions has roots in the American past. Once before, accelerated technological change, and its inevitable concomitant social change, placed the established democratic value pattern of American society in grave jeopardy; educators and social workers then joined the combination of forces that mobilized to maintain it.

Following the Civil War, the thrusts of intensive industrialization and urbanization accelerated the transformation of America; the factory and the city became the dominant landmarks of the American scene. As today, changes set off a series of repercussive waves within the social system. One of these waves had come in the form of a powerful urban draw: a pull toward the city. Both industrial expansion and urban draw had been allowed free play because legitimate regulative authority was inhibited by the insistence of dominant groups in society that the classical economic doctrine of laissez-faire applied also to social policy.

Consequently, little or no planning was done to anticipate the social consequences of a rapidly expanding industrial and urban culture. As new cities sprang up, and older cities assumed a metropolitan scale, an ethic of catch-as-catch-can displaced traditional human values in the American social environment. Cities were turned into jungles teeming with defenseless human prey in the form of newly arrived immigrants and rural folk lured to the city by job opportunities in the factory and by the glitter of city lights.

The institutional network that links social values with the formal structure of society broke down at many points under the impact. Certain sectors of American society, however, refused to accept pockmarking social and economic ills as the promise of American life. By reasserting the primacy of democratic and humanistic values in American society, they attacked the laissez-faire attitudes that were eroding traditional values. They set out to regulate the institutional flywheel of society to a tempo better suited to the new life of cities and factories.

The early years of the twentieth century provided numerous instances of collaboration between educators and social workers in efforts to adapt the engines of social democracy to the exigencies of a new age. What today are called the "helping professions" began to assume a bolder posture in the day-to-day affairs of city life. Many social workers recognized a responsibility beyond that of "dispensers of band-aids" for gushing arteries; instead they viewed themselves as agents of social change. When they also had to dispense "band-aids," it was to save individuals and family groups from sinking into the lower depths. Social Darwinism was for them more than a theoretical abstraction. Each day brought them a close look at its social and economic consequences in the tenements and sweatshops of the city.

It was Lillian Wald who began, in 1902, the school nurse program in New York public schools by sending, as an experiment, a Henry Street Settlement House nurse to a public school. And when M. G. Brumbaugh, superintendent of schools in Philadelphia, stood before the 1908 Annual Convention of the National Education Association and exhorted: "We must, as educators, take our stand with those that oppose the coining of the blood of children into the currency of the market place," leaders from the young profession of social work were giving voice to similar exhortations before other sections of the same NEA convention. The two professions were joined at that time in the demand for child labor laws and the enforcement of compulsory school attendance. Jane Addams, Robert W. Bruce, then Secretary of the New York Committee on the Physical Welfare of School Children, and Florence Kelley were also on that 1908 program of the NEA.

Present-day Needs

The communication challenge which this conference has brought into sharp focus for the two professions is a component of the same larger challenge which, at the dawn of the twentieth century, had brought together educators and social workers as collaborators in a common cause. Objective conditions in contemporary society now compel education and social work to collaborate again in the same common cause.

Now, however, collaboration has to be more sophisticated. Past collaboration must be continued in the sphere of social policy formation. But in response to modern-day imperatives, education and social work will have to engage in interprofessional collaboration at the point of rendering service to clients they share in common. Here, at the point of rendering service, is where the communication challenge has relevance.

As Boehm demonstrated, sophisticated collaboration at the point of rendering service in the public school organization generates a thrust for a corresponding sophistication in the communications network between education and social work. Boehm illustrated a traditional view of the public school organization in which it is meaningful to talk of interaction between a teacher and a social worker employed by a school system. Efficient administative co-ordination and a relatively simple communications network can make such interaction effective. But there is a second concept of school organization in which it is no longer meaningful to speak of a teacher interacting with a school social worker. Now the teacher's interaction has to be with a variety of professionals, in and out of school and society, in planned interaction.

It is immediately apparent that the conventional communications network of the public school organization is grossly inadequate for such a view of public school services. The question of who will co-ordinate the education and social work services arises at once. Of course, should planned interaction become the pattern of school organization, an adaption will have to be effected in educational technology and administrative process.

According to Talcott Parsons' general theory of social systems, "the primary reference point for the linkage of values through legitimation with the structure of the social system is institutionalization." [1] However, even after values are so endowed with institutional muscle, they still have no automatic way of fulfilling themselves. They require formal structures; that is, administrative organizations. The goal structures of formal organizations become, therefore, respositories of social values. These values are the legitimate sources for all formal organizations in society; for their technologies and functional patterns of operation, and for the demands which they have to make upon community resources. Following Parsons, society, as a total social system, depends upon its network of formal organizations for the necessary technological processes which facilitate the adaptation of its institutionalized value system to new conditions and, therefore, the survival of society itself.

In the past, educators and social workers have provided the requisite skills for the incorporation of emerging subvalues into the goal structures of their respective professional organizations and, thereby, have facilitated in these two sectors of social action the adaptation of American society to the new milieu of the early twentieth century. Through innovations in structure and process, they harnessed natural response to change in these two professions with administrative rationality. The comprehensive high school, junior college, junior high school, the Visiting Nurses Association, well-baby clinics, family and children's bureaus, the American model of the neighborhood settlement house, and others are inventions of institutional perspective in another age.

ADMINISTRATIVE PROBLEMS

However, since that period, there has been a loss of institutional

---

[1] Talcott Parsons, *Structure and Process in Modern Societies* (New York: Free Press of Glencoe, 1963), p. 177.

perspective in education and social work. In the preparation of administrators, for example, professional programs have perhaps been producing replicas of the "bureaucratic virtuoso" rather than institutional leaders for the administrative organizations of public education and social work.[2]

Moreover, the harmony that Boehm has identified as the critical requisite for effective collaboration has continued to elude education and social work. It will continue to elude the two professions until those at all structural levels of the public school organization —and not merely those at the managerial level—internalize Durkheim's dictum that society is the very source of educational life.[3]

The verity of Durkheim's dictum is acknowledged at many points in Sand's definition of the profession of teaching as a function of society. Therefore, when Boehm's reference to the public school as "an organ of social change" is juxtaposed with Sand's paper, it strikes the challenge of this conference. For in the main, to speak of today's public school as an organ of social change is to recite a hollow shibboleth.

In the division of labor within the professions of education and social work, society has ascribed to schools of education and social work the differentiated function of preparing students for the professional roles that are required to attain the goals of the public school system and the social welfare agency. However, entry into any professional role turns on more than the mere acquisition of process skills. The internalization of professional values, learning normative role behavior, a personal commitment to the profession as, following Merton's conceptualization, a "cosmopolitan" are some of the other important components of role socialization in a profession. In professional service organizations these value variables are especially crucial, if conflict with clients is to be avoided.

In the New York City public schools, for example, an estimated 90 percent of the teachers are predominantly middle class in aspirations and values, while students are distributed about 60 percent lower class, 30 percent lower-middle class, and only 10 percent upper-middle and upper class. This means that over half the children are in direct contact with teachers whose values and ideas differ from their own.[4]

---

[2] The concept of the "bureaucratic virtuoso" appears in Robert K. Merton's classic study of the bureaucratic personality, "Bureaucratic Structure and Personality" in Merton, *Social Theory and Social Structure* (rev. ed.; Glencoe, Ill.: Free Press, 1957), p. 199.

[3] Emile Durkheim, *Education and Sociology*, trans. by Sherwood D. Fox (Glencoe, Ill.: Free Press, 1956), p. 132.

[4] *See* Samuel H. Popper, "The High School in the War on Poverty," *Bulletin of the National Association of Secondary School Principals*, Vol. 46, No. 273 (April 1962), pp. 90–95.

The Challenge

Can there be two social groups in society set more perfectly on a collision course? Sociologists, who specialize in the study of conflict in organizations, see here a rich harvest from the seeds of "relative deprivation." Merely providing more education is not enough. Indeed, T. R. Fyvel in *Troublemakers* attributes lower-class alienation in England to an increase of educational opportunities in postwar Britain. He does not refer to the concept of relative deprivation, but in theoretical terms that is precisely the phenomenon he is reporting.[5]

SOCIAL AND PSYCHOLOGICAL FOUNDATIONS

Study in the social and psychological foundations of education is expected to endow teachers with a conceptual capacity for containing value conflict which inhibits effective teacher-pupil interaction. On this note, Quillen and Gage have brought into sight the Achilles heel in preparation programs of all professional role incumbents in the public school organization.

The area of social foundations of education seems to suffer the greater hardship. Quillen traced the struggle of social foundations for a status in the school of education. Social scientists for the most part had turned their backs on social foundations in professional education. Things are a bit brighter today, but even now, when there is a flowering in the social sciences, Quillen looks to the next generation when "competence in the social sciences and a knowledge of professional education can be combined in more individuals."

Psychological foundations, on the other hand, have fared much better. Ever since the days of William Jame's *Talks to Teachers,* educational psychology has been getting an ever increasing share of school of education budgets. Educational psychology is most important but what seems to be wrong in the content of psychological foundations today is its neglect of social psychology in favor of cognitive theory and cognitive motivation.

Cognitive motivation, of course, is very important in teaching and calls for the exercise of sophisticated psychological skill. But where, if not in psychological foundations, will teachers master the psychological skill of stimulating in pupils an affective response to educational process and to the school environment? And without a prior affective response to the school itself, the most painstaking efforts at cognitive motivation are wasted. It is in psychological foundations that teachers master that vital empathetic skill which, in the hands of a skilled classroom teacher, could initiate

---

5 T. R. Fyvel, *Troublemakers: Rebellious Youth in an Affluent Society* (New York: Schocken Books, 1962).

the transformation of a potentially wasted American into a socially useful American.

EMPATHETIC SKILLS

The ability to empathize with a client without a surrender of professional objectivity is a precious skill of the social worker. Empathy, joined by other technical skills, enables the school social worker to complete the transformation that the classroom teacher had begun.

This social dimension of a teacher's role is difficult to capture in a preparation program that emerged in the nineteenth century, and to which too many schools of education still adhere. Nevertheless, without the exercise of empathetic skill, the modern-day teacher in the school organization no longer can fulfill the expectations of society. Effective role performance by the teacher can no longer be attained in this age without a fusion of social, psychological, and cognitive perspectives. How ironic, therefore, is the low estate of social foundations in so many of our schools of education and the lack of social psychology in psychological foundations; these two areas of teacher preparation have the necessary conceptual tools to effect the fusion.

CHANGING TEACHERS' ROLES

Compounding the irony is the fact that those persons in the public school organization who must assume primary responsibility for improvement and innovation in educational technology have been aware for a long time of the imperatives for integrating social, psychological, and cognitive dimensions in the teacher's role. The slow-paced response in teacher education to these modern-day imperatives is an illustration of "trained incapacity" in teacher preparation programs. Because faculties in schools of education have so completely accepted nineteenth-century norms of teacher education, they have difficulty in effecting necessary adaptive responses to emerging professional imperatives.

The following two passages from the 1951 Yearbook of the Association for Supervision and Curriculum Development illustrate the point and validate the theme of the conference.

The first of these passages focuses on the teacher's role and notes:

> The accepted role of the teacher in American society has passed through two stages and is now entering a third. The first accepted role was to teach a specific kind and amount of subject matter to a group or groups of children. This role was fairly adequate when children and youth learned outside of school most of the things they needed to know to get along in society. The major reason for having a school was to help

pupils to become literate so that they could learn through books those things they were unable to learn through direct experiences. The second stage charged the teacher with responsibility for teaching children as persons. Acceptance of this responsibility was brought about largely through the influence of psychologists and the introduction of extra-curricular activities in the schools. Of course, the teacher under this concept continued to teach subject matter, but he went beyond that. This concept gave recognition for the first time to the wholeness of learning. The third stage which is just emerging has its roots in the community school concept. It charges the teacher with responsibility for helping both directly and indirectly to improve living in the community in which the school is located. The teacher under this concept teaches subject matter and children, but goes beyond that to work with the community as a whole in the improvement of living for all in the community.[6]

The second passage offers a functional definition of the teacher's role in the context of modern society:

To contribute effectively to improvement of community living, the teacher must learn to perform three broad functions. The first of these is to teach one or more groups of children, subject matter to be drawn upon, and methods to be used will be different as the major forces in society . . . change. Knowledge about human development as it increases also will change both the content and method used in teaching a group of children. The second function is to contribute to improvement of the total educational program of the school to which the teacher accepts assignment. To do this the teacher must be part of a team, each member of which accepts the appropriate share of responsibility for the success of the whole faculty. The teacher will realize that improvements by him will be relatively ineffective unless other members of the same faculty are making similar improvements. He will recognize that curriculum improvements are unitary in much the same way that learning on the parts of pupils is whole. The third function is to work with individuals and groups in the community in efforts to improve community living. This does not mean that the school takes over and reforms the community. It does mean that the school, through its staff and facilities, should help to make the community sensitive to its needs for improvement, and stand ready to help at all times.[7]

---

6 W. E. Armstrong, *et al.,* "Conditions Compelling Curriculum Change," in *Action for Curriculum Improvement, Yearbook of the Association for Supervision and Curriculum Development* (Washington, D.C.: Association for Supervision and Curriculum Development, 1951), pp. 33–34.

7 *Ibid.,* p. 34.

The foregoing functional definition of the teacher's role bespeaks the growing sophistication in educational process. But it does more than that. It defines in functional terms the role of the teacher in the emerging urban community school, a concept of the public school to which much discussion was devoted at the conference.

PLANNED COLLABORATION

It had become patently clear at the conference that failure to collaborate and to communicate with one another in the emerging community school jeopardizes the role integrity of both the teacher and the school social worker. When the communications network of a complex social system is inadequate, role definition is difficult to attain, role expectations become exaggerated, or otherwise distorted, and an excessive flow of demand in the direction of a given person can lead to a total breakdown of role.

The concept of the community school demands an integrated communications network. This cannot be obtained from nineteenth-century teacher education programs. The emerging network of interactions which is in fact turning the public school into an improvised expression of the community school concept has evolved in the crucible of twentieth-century problems and is beyond the ken of the nineteenth-century models of teacher education. The high incidence of "reality shock" among recent entrants into professional education, and the concomitant dropouts of teachers, is powerful empirical evidence of the inadequacy and antiquity of modern-day preparation programs for technical roles in the public school organization.

Future Directions

It is clear that the inescapable urgency for interprofessional collaboration between education and social work cannot stop at social foundations. Programs such as Mobilization For Youth in New York, Community Progress, Inc., in New Haven, and Youth for Service in San Francisco are examples of temporary structures with which American society is responding to the onset of grave social problems. Out of these temporary structures permanent forms will inevitably emerge in which close collaboration between educational process and social work process will be a primary imperative. In sum if teachers are to be effective in the classroom, teachers and social workers had better become familiar with one another's process under planned conditions. Should they fail to plan for such a collaboration, they shall, in any event, be forced to learn more about one another's process but in a diffused and ad hoc fashion.

The Challenge

The two professions risk the censure of society if this conference does not result in a steadfast resolve to maintain the momentum of the planned collaboration. The conference has defined the contours of a many-sided problem which now confronts the professions of education and social work. Education and social work have collaborated in the past and society was the better for it. But whereas past collaborations for the most part had taken the form of improvised responses to emerging social problems, future collaboration will have to be planned and aimed at the release of creative initiative in the two professions.

AREAS OF COLLABORATION

It is clear from all that has transpired at the conference that effective interprofessional collaboration between education and social work will have to begin in the school of education and the school of social work. It is no accident that the invitation list to this conference consisted almost exclusively of deans and professors from schools of education and social work. For these two systems have the primary and inescapable responsibility in the division of labor for endowing members of our professions with the concepts and processes which are required for practice.

Clearly, the collaboration between these two systems has to move beyond an occasional exchange of faculty for service on doctoral examining committees. Enterprising ventures into joint appointments to senior faculty ranks in social and psychological foundations will have to be explored, and without the petty tyrannies that now befall an incumbent of a joint appointment at increment and promotion periods. Experienced academicians are wary of such joint appointments at this time and the unwary, more likely than not, lack the needed experience for such appointments.

Long and hard study shall have to be given to the courses in social and psychological foundations of education, with perhaps one social foundations sequence for both education and social work. Fresh ideas and new instructional methodologies in social foundations are sorely needed. As for psychological foundations, the Division of Educational Psychology of the American Psychological Association is already at work. No doubt other academic disciplines with a stake in this area of teacher education would be willing to set up similar committees. Perhaps a task force of specialists drawn from philosophy, psychology, sociology, communications media, education, social work, and other relevant professional and academic fields might be constituted to assault this problem.

Effective simulation of reality could also be an ideal method of bringing together advanced students in schools of education and

170

social work. This would not be an imitation of simulation materials now used in educational administration, but a research project, jointly undertaken by education and social work, out of which would come simulated instructional materials of a wide variety based upon empirically ascertained criteria for success of school personnel who function at the service-rendering level of education.

There might be fruitful collaboration between schools of education and social work in the area of supervised practice-teaching. Because the supervised practice-teaching experience is, in fact, the internship stage just prior to formal entry into the profession of education, it need not be limited to the classroom. Especially at this time, when teacher education is moving fast in the direction of a five-year program, the scope of supervised practice-teaching might be enlarged by experiences in a settlement house, family and children's agency, child-guidance clinic, and so forth. Perhaps this is one way of helping education gain some of the insights of social work.

There is little point in speculating further at this time about the procedural means of transforming the substantive meaning of the conference into an action program. The foregoing suggestions were only illustrations of the types of procedures discussed during the conference. Once the task of designing an action program is begun, all sorts of serendipital advantages will be discovered.

This Interprofessional Conference has already set the stage for a collaboration between social work and education. As a next step, perhaps the leadership of the National Association of Social Workers and the Council on Social Work Education could initiate discussions with the leadership of relevant educational groups for the following threefold purpose:

1. To explore the feasibility of a joint commission to formulate a multidimensional program for research and development.
2. Given such a joint commission, and a program design, task forces could then be activated to fulfill specific segments of the program. The joint commission would co-ordinate these forces and otherwise perform entrepreneurial tasks.
3. To seek jointly funds from government or private sources to support the program.

Still another avenue of approach might be through the University Council for Educational Administration, which has established excellent channels of communication with the U.S. Office of Education, with professional organizations in education, and with the lay National School Boards Association. These and others, such as the National Commission on Teacher Education and Professional

Standards, the American Association of Colleges for Teacher Education, and the National Council for Accreditation of Teacher Education would also have to become involved at many points in such a collaboration.

The National School Boards Association, which is not a professional body, stands for the legal link between the authority source of the community and the school organization. The boards of education are the official policy-making bodies in the public schools, not the superintendents or principals. Therefore, all efforts to make of the school an effective organ of social change will be dogged by frustration unless the institutional level of school structure is joined with the technical and managerial levels in support of these efforts.

These are illustrative of the strategies that might be attempted to continue the collaboration between education and social work that was begun at the conference. No doubt there are other strategies. Now that the social and professional imperatives for collaboration have been brought into focus, education and social work dare not settle for anything less than planned collaboration in the future.

It was suggested at the beginning of this response that the substantive meaning of the conference has been a determination in the professional sectors of education and social work to conserve the institutionalized value system of American society in a period of vast and rapid transformations. The following passage from the literature of educational administration is, therefore, appropriate at this juncture:

> If, as H. G. Wells noted, human history becomes more and more a race between education and catastrophe, a history written half a century from now could record either of two conclusions: that education is winning out because the human race has greatly improved its lot and the prospects for its future, or that catastrophe is rapidly overwhelming humanity because education has been neglected or has become the tool of some selfish and ruthless group or groups.[8]

In professional collaboration the contributions of education and social work can help to facilitate national integration and thus keep catastrophe from overwhelming society. Let the record of this conference stand as a joint manifesto of a resolve to engage in planned collaboration toward this end.

---

8 Theodore L. Reller and Edgar L. Morphet, *Comparative Educational Administration* (Englewood Cliffs, N.J.: Prentice-Hall, 1962), p. 1.

CONFERENCE
PARTICIPANTS

The positions given were held by the participants at the time of the conference.

HILDA C. M. ARNDT, Professor and Co-ordinator of Field Work, School of Social Welfare, Louisiana State University, Baton Rouge, Louisiana.

HELEN C. BAILEY, Visiting Professor, Graduate School of Education, University of Pennsylvania, Philadelphia, Pennsylvania.

ROBERT H. BECK, Professor, College of Education, University of Minnesota, Minneapolis, Minnesota.

JACK W. BIRCH, Associate Dean and Professor, School of Education, University of Pittsburgh, Pittsburgh, Pennsylvania.

WERNER W. BOEHM, Dean, Graduate School of Social Work, Rutgers —The State University, New Brunswick, New Jersey.

OPAL BOSTON, Director, School Social Work Program, Indianapolis Public Schools, Indianapolis, Indiana.

ROBERT L. BRACKENBURY, Professor, School of Education, University of Southern California, Los Angeles, California.

CHARLES B. BRINK, Dean, School of Social Work, University of Washington, Seattle, Washington.

DAN H. COOPER, Professor, School of Education, University of Michigan, Ann Arbor, Michigan.

VIRGINIA BEALL DeLONG, Principal, J. K. Lilly Senior School No. 53, Indianapolis, Indiana.

ROBERT S. FISK, Dean, School of Education, State University of New York at Buffalo, Buffalo, New York.

N. L. GAGE, Professor, School of Education, Stanford University, Stanford, California.

ROSE GREEN, Professor, School of Social Work, University of Southern California, Los Angeles, California.

173

Conference Participants

MARGARET E. HARTFORD, Associate Professor of Social Work, School of Applied Social Sciences, Western Reserve University, Cleveland, Ohio.

ERASMUS L. HOCH, Professor of Psychology, University of Michigan, Ann Arbor, Michigan.

MARGARET E. HOFFMAN, Professor, Graduate School of Social Work, University of Denver, Denver, Colorado.

JOSEPH P. HOURIHAN, Professor, School of Social Work, Wayne State University, Detroit, Michigan.

ARLIEN JOHNSON, Dean Emeritus, School of Social Work, University of Southern California, Los Angeles, California.

KENNETH W. KINDELSPERGER, Dean, Raymond A. Kent School of Social Work, University of Louisville, Louisville, Kentucky.

GORDON C. LEE, Dean, College of Education, University of Washington, Seattle, Washington.

BOYD R. McCANDLESS, Chairman, Department of Special Education, and Director, Center for the Study of Child Development, School of Education, Indiana University, Bloomington, Indiana.

JOHN McDOWELL, Dean, School of Social Work, Boston University, Boston, Massachusetts.

LAWRENCE F. MERL, Chairman, Council on Social Work in the Schools, National Association of Social Workers, and Assistant Professor, School of Social Work, University of Minnesota, Minneapolis, Minnesota.

BARBARA M. MOORE, Associate Director, Department of Social Work Practice, National Association of Social Workers, New York, New York.

HELEN NORTHEN, Professor, School of Social Work, University of Southern California, Los Angeles, California.

FLORENCE POOLE, The Jane Addams Graduate School of Social Work, University of Illinois, Chicago, Illinois.

SAMUEL H. POPPER, Associate Professor, College of Education, University of Minnesota, Minneapolis, Minnesota.

I. JAMES QUILLEN, Dean and Professor, School of Education, Stanford University, Stanford, California.

THEODORE RELLER, Dean, School of Education, University of California, Berkeley, California.

GWEN RETHERFORD, Professor, College of Education, Wayne State University, Detroit, Michigan.

J. WILLIAM RIOUX, Specialist for School Social Work, Office of Education, U.S. Department of Health, Education, and Welfare, Washington, D.C.

OLE SAND, Director, Center for the Study of Instruction, National Education Association, Washington, D.C.

MILDRED SIKKEMA, Consultant on Educational Standards, Council on Social Work Education, New York, New York.

RUTH E. SMALLEY, Dean and Professor, School of Social Work, University of Pennsylvania, Philadelphia, Pennsylvania.

LOUISE C. SPENCE, District Administrator and Supervisor of District Services, Division of Children and Youth, State Department of Public Welfare, Madison, Wisconsin.

MARGERY THOMPSON, Program Specialist, Center for the Study of Instruction, National Education Association, Washington, D.C.

WALTER B. WAETJEN, General Director, Interprofessional Research Commission on Pupil Personnel Services, Bureau of Educational Research and Field Services, University of Maryland, College Park, Maryland.

ROBERT WASSER, Field Work Consultant, School of Social Welfare, University of California, Berkeley, California.

JANE WILLE, Consultant and Associate Professor, The Jane Addams Graduate School of Social Work, University of Illinois, Chicago, Illinois.

5M/SSW/8–65